change the script runnir
is crucial to your health
The "renewal of your min
transformation. Dr. Phil

Body of Christ by address...g this very personal issue
head on. I recommend this book to you.

—DR. LARRY K. ASPLUND
VICE PRESIDENT FOR ACADEMIC AFFAIRS
CLST LEARNING INSTITUTE

As you explore the pages of *The Most Powerful Voice in Your Life*, you will discover a life changing tool to help you move from a less defeated mindset to a more daily victorious way of living. Over the years that I have known Dr. Phil, I find TRUTH in the messages he shares. In reviewing this book, my ears are now open to a more powerful and encouraging tool to use in my own self talk. Let the Holy Spirit transform your listening ears as you read this awesome gift Dr. Phil has unfolded so simply for you.

—REV. BARBARA A. SCHULZ
PRESIDENT WESTERN BIBLE COLLEGE IN PHOENIX,
ARIZONA; GENERAL PRESBYTER, THE GENERAL
COUNCIL OF THE ASSEMBLIES OF GOD

My friend Dr. Phil Willingham has written a message of hope, mind renewal and victory! In his new book, *The Most Powerful Voice In Your Life* the reader will be taken on a journey of freedom and new found authority over the lies of Satan! As I read through the pages I thought to myself how many times I have battled the destructive thoughts and the feeling of lost hope that can consume even God's most mature leaders. This book is transformational and written from a man with his finger on the pulse of this generation! This is a must-read for all believers.

—PAT SCHATZLINE
EVANGELIST, REMNANT MINISTRIES INTERNATIONAL
AUTHOR OF *WHY IS GOD SO MAD AT ME?*,
I AM REMNANT, & *UNQUALIFIED*

I am thrilled to recommend Phil Willingham's book, entitled, *The Most Powerful Voice in Your Life*. Pastor Willingham and I have partnered together in ministry and I have witnessed firsthand in his life the kind of multiplying, positive leadership that he writes about in this book. This valuable resource will give you the action steps to making the rest of your life the most fulfilling possible.

—DAVID SOBREPENA
WORD OF HOPE
FOUNDING PASTOR
MANILA, PHILIPPINES

Words are the outward expressions of the inward thoughts of a person. In *The Most Powerful Voice in Your Life*, Phil Willingham teaches us how to retrain our thinking in order to develop a positive inspirational mindset that will attract the most positive outcomes possible in our lives. Be sure to purchase your copy of *The Most Powerful Voice in Your Life* today!

—ELMER L. TOWNS
LIBERTY UNIVERSITY
COFOUNDER

Small thinkers make big stinkers! Phil Willingham teaches us the necessary path of sowing our thoughts and growing our lives. *The Most Powerful Voice in Your Life*, will equip you and your team to survive, strive, and succeed through life's greatest challenges, coming your way in the future. This book will catapult your thoughts many years ahead of your current life and will save you countless hours toward achieving your personal goals.

—JAMES O. DAVIS
COFOUNDER-BILLION SOUL NETWORK
FOUNDER-CUTTING EDGE INTERNATIONAL

Phil Willingham's latest book, *The Most Powerful Voice In Your Life* is a must read for all visionary leaders who seek to exponentially compound the impact of their lives in the years to come. Every Christian leader will greatly benefit from the insights and applications in most valuable resource. Be sure to read it and get extra copies for your peers!

—DR. MICHAEL KNIGHT
FOUNDER GLOBAL COACHING NETWORK
NATIONAL CHURCH PLANTING CHURCH OF GOD

Dr. Willingham's book is very needed in the church today. The subject and struggles of self-talk are everywhere, but no one seems to talk about it. Dr. Willingham's voice on this vital subject offers Biblical guidance and hope to all of us. This book will help you answer your worst critic, yourself."

—PASTOR TIM WALK
HIGH SCHOOL PASTOR
@MOUNT PARAN CHURCH IN ATLANTA GEORGIA

This book by Dr. Willingham is a FRESH, NEW APPROACH, to an age old problem. It is not simply another book dealing with the powers of positive thinking, but a practical spiritual path to becoming all that God has said you can become. I believe this book will be a tool to help many, many OVERCOME debilitating thinking by learning, as Dr. Willingham outlines, to "STOP" speaking failure to our own lives. Then, to "START" adapting a LIFESTYLE, of guarding and mastering, what our OWN inner voice is saying, deep within our own hearts. "Truly, life and death, and success or failure, is in the life of our own tongue." Thank you Phil, for sharing this book with this generation, and the many generations to come.

—Dennis Wilson
International Song Writer and Artist

Dr. Phil provides a comprehensive and unique discussion recognizing the existence of our inner monologue. The reader is not only made cognizant of the influence of "self talk" and its consequences (possibly repercussions), but is also offered pragmatic and biblical guidance to modify his or her response to it. It is impressive to consider the applicability of this topic to all individuals regardless of position, status, or circumstance. I highly recommend the reading of this book.

—Attorney Adam J. Moore
Personal friend

THE MOST
POWERFUL
VOICE
IN YOUR LIFE

THE MOST
POWERFUL
VOICE
IN YOUR LIFE

Learn to Tame Your Self-Talk

DR. PHIL WILLINGHAM

BILLIONSOUL
PUBLISHING

Published by Billion Soul Publishing
100 Alexandria Blvd.
Suite 9
Oviedo, FL 32765

www.billionsoulpub.com

Printed in the United States of America.

Dedication

MANY PEOPLE, TOO many to list, have influenced my thinking and my life through the years that helped shape this book.

I dedicated this book to the church I have the joy and privilege of pastoring over that last 14 years.

To my loving and caring wife, Rhonda, anybody who knows me understands how much I adore and appreciate her. She has been my greatest encourager in life since I first met her when we were both teens 40 years ago. If everything else in my life all went away, I'd be okay as long as I knew she would still be by my side.

To my three gifted children, Sunshine, Matthew, Amber and my five grandsons Mason, Jeremiah, Jake, Tray, and Charley. I love you dearly! I've learned so much from you all about life and love and what matters most.

Finally, I save the best until last. I am so thankful to my heavenly Father for entrusting me with the life and ministry He has given to me. May all the good that comes from this book exalt and honor Him.

Contents

The core of true success is love.
And that includes loving yourself
enough to take care of yourself.

ZIG ZIGLAR

Introduction

AFTER FORTY YEARS of ministry I still find it heartbreaking when I meet people who live defeated, despite the power and work of Christ. The truth is, they deserve more. You deserve more. We all do.

Why do people live in bondage or with a lack of faith or joy or freedom, even though Christ has promised more? They live defeated lives not because the Bible is not true or victory has not been promised, but because they never take control of their own self talk. Our words are the words that define our inner worlds, our minds, and our hearts. Proverbs 4:23 commands us to guard it. Guard your heart, for it is the wellspring from which all life flows. Imagine that. God has commanded us to guard our hearts and to protect our lives from negative and toxic words, images, and worldly noise.

I have personally discovered that the most powerful voice in my life is not the voice of my parents, friends, spouse, or even God. The most powerful voice in my life is my own self talk. While I grew up in a Christian home and heard about God's willingness and ability to change my life, I struggled to overcome my own destructive self talk. While I received much outside encouragement from my parents and others about my ability to work with my hands and get a job done, when it came to my ability to do well in school, I remember hearing teacher after teacher say, "Phil struggles." Even at a young age, my self talk sounded like this: "You will not pass this test," or "This work is too hard to understand," or "Your best option is to learn a skill because education is not your field." This negative self talk led me to quit school at the age of sixteen. It would be fourteen years later, at the age of thirty, that I would go back to school, get my GED, and finally begin my educational journey. This journey would conclude with two Master of Divinity degrees, one Master of Theology degree, and a DMin at age fifty. Was the journey easy? Did I suddenly become a genius? Absolutely not. What did change was the way that I talked to myself. Instead of saying things like "I can't" or "I will never be able," I started saying, "I can do this…I am capable of learning this…I will finish this." Again, the most powerful voice to which you will listen is your own…your self talk.

Of course, eliminating negative self talk and developing positive self talk is not a one-time decision but an ongoing process. In fact, over the last forty-two years of ministry, I have had to confront and attack negative thoughts and words countless times.

One such incident occurred a few years ago when I was in a time of ministry transition. Having just been voted out of a church, I found myself struggling to keep a positive perspective. I had worked at some type of job since I was eight years old, either farm work or construction, but at the age of forty-five I was unemployed. To keep the family going and the bills paid, I took a construction job. One day, needing a break from the hot, southern temperatures, I went into a fast food restaurant. A group of local pastors whom I knew came in together as I drank my cup of water. As these men ordered and then sat down across the room, I started talking to myself. I was talking negatively to myself because of my situation. Instead of relying on God, talking positively, and praying, a negative conversation blossomed in my mind.

In this book I mention "stinkin' thinkin'." It is a mindset that says over and over, "I stink, you stink, life stinks." So right there in that fast-food restaurant, my mind began to tell me, "I stink." In other words, I am worthless. If I were a better leader, if I were a better pastor, if I were... I kept this up until I shifted to "You stink." In other words, nobody loves me. In my mind I started attacking the ministers: "They see me sitting over here in my dirty work clothes. They don't care about me. They are ashamed of me. I should go over there and give them a piece of my mind." But at that point, I realized that I didn't have many pieces of my mind left, so I thought I better hold on to what I had.

My self talk was taking me straight down. I was having a pity party, and nobody was attending but me, myself, and I! Then my mind shifted to "Life stinks." At that moment I had to make a decision. Would I continue down this road of negative self talk, or would I take control of my thoughts? I determined at that moment not to allow my thoughts to defeat me. I got up from where I was sitting, walked over to the pastors, and engaged them in a conversation. As I walked those twenty feet to their table, I talked to myself: "Phil, this is just a season in your life. Where you are now doesn't mean that is where you will stay. God's calling and hand is on your life, and another ministry opportunity is coming your way."

By the time I arrived at their table, those "I stink, you stink, life stinks" thoughts had been taken captive, and I was thinking on those things that were true, honorable, just, lovely, and pure. When I left the restaurant that day, I still faced some negative circumstances and uncertainty about my future, but I was confident that positive self talk would help me maintain a better outlook on life than negative self talk.

It is my desire to help others discover this destructive self talk in their lives and to teach them how to control it by training themselves to defeat those negative voices. In this book I will challenge you to stop and listen to your self talk and become aware of how words and conversations are like elevators. They can take us up, or they can take us down. Because we often are not aware of this self talk, it needs to be pointed out, and we need to pay attention.

This book will encourage parents, spouses, teenagers, and everyone in between to stop and consider how their thoughts impact their lives and the lives of others.

How's your self talk?

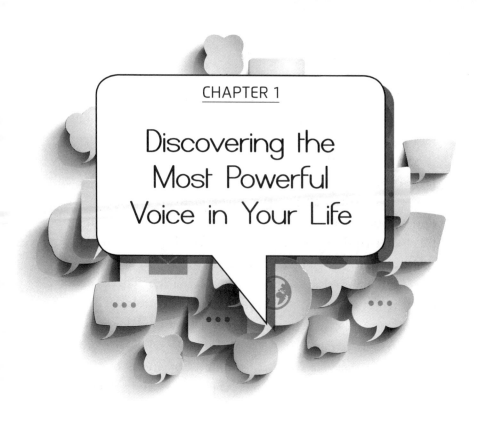

CHAPTER 1

Discovering the Most Powerful Voice in Your Life

D O YOU TALK to yourself?

Of course you do... we all do at different times and in various situations.

Kids do it, teenagers do it, even adults do it.

We've all seen a toddler as she looks at a red puzzle piece and says, "This red piece goes into this round hole." She says this to herself, and then she begins to operate on that assumption. When it doesn't fit, she gets frustrated. As we get older, we stop talking out loud to ourselves, fearing that people might think something is wrong with us.

Our oldest daughter, Sunshine, was born with Down syndrome. Down syndrome children have a very candid way of self talking. I don't know if you have ever been around many Down's children, but like Sunshine they have a way of communicating that shows. When Sunshine feels frustrated or fearful or sad, she will self talk. This is true for a lot of children with Down syndrome.

Let me give you an example. Sometimes we will ask her to do something that she doesn't want to do. But she is not like an average teenager or any average person who will stand and argue with you. She will go upstairs, shut her door, and for the next five or ten minutes, she will self talk. You can stand by the door and listen as she has a long conversation with herself.

Because of the speech impediment in Down's children, they typically can't communicate very well, so they self talk in order to work out their fears and frustrations. Sometimes Sunshine creates an imaginary friend, or she might talk about her "cousins" always being with her.

After Sunshine has been upstairs for awhile talking to herself, she will eventually come back downstairs, look at me or her mom, and say, "Okay, I'll do it. Brian (her make-believe friend) told me it's okay."

That's simply self talk at work.

We're not all like Sunshine. Most of us have self talk hidden in our subconscious. So how do we identify it?

Some studies show that our normal rate of talking is about 120 words per minute, but we can think at the rate of 1,300 words a minute. Consider the result. No wonder some of us get so depressed when we dwell on our problems. Can you imagine just ten minutes of negative self talk? That's ten minutes of thinking about how bad your life is. That's 13,000 destructive, discouraging words being pumped into your spirit every ten minutes.

Self talk is powerful.

Sometimes people say, "Hey, don't worry. Be happy!" We all know that is often easier said than done. Like me, perhaps, many of you find yourselves upset and anxious as you lay down at night. Instead of falling asleep, all of those negative self thoughts start running through your mind. You start thinking to yourself, "Why did I say that? Why did I do that today? How am I going to pay my bills? How am I going to...?" Can anybody relate to that? That's simply self talk.

Now here is the great news—God understands you. He is the one who created you, He made you, He formed you, He knows how you work, and He understands how powerful your self talk can be. I am here to tell you that there is no level of spirituality which you can reach where you won't have to battle negative self talk. Some people think, "Well, if I were just more spiritual, or if I were just more mature, then I would never have any negative self talk. I would always be positive and say positive things and believe positive things." This is simply not so. If you think you have to reach a certain level of spirituality or maturity, my friend, you are going to create a lot of confusion in your life.

Only you can identify and be responsible for the words you tell yourself each day, week, month, and year. Only you have the power to control the way you think and talk to yourself. God is there for you. God created you to be more and do greater. The key is to recognize when you're not talking to yourself the way He would.

The most powerful voice in the universe to any one person is his or her own self talk.

ACTION POINTS

1. Before you go on to the next chapter, identify how self talk has a negative impact on your life.

2. Recognize and identify how much time you spend talking negative words to yourself rather than positive words.

3. How can you take responsibility for your thoughts and begin to bring them in line with God's Word?

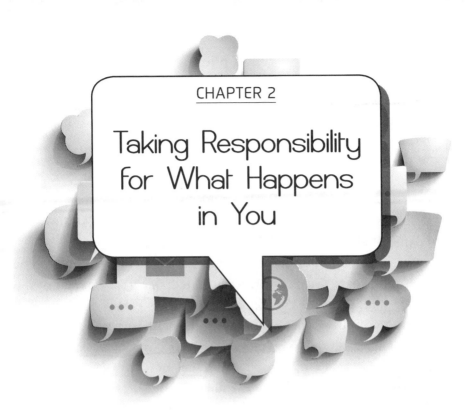

CHAPTER 2

Taking Responsibility for What Happens in You

THE HUMAN MIND can override most things, including the voice of God. Often it doesn't even matter if your faith is strong or your awareness of God's call is clear. Self-talk can sabotage an individual's walk and destiny. Without the confidence to take action, you simply won't. If you talk yourself out of success, it's an issue within your own mind. The solution? Be aware, take thoughts captive, and meditate on powerful Scriptures.

Do you understand that your self-talk voice is more powerful than any other voice in your life? Do you understand that your voice, which includes what you do and what you say to yourself, is usually even louder than what God says to you?

In 2 Timothy 1:7, the Bible says, "I've not given you the spirit of fear, but the spirit of power and love and a sound mind." Yet for many of us, our own voices tell us that we are afraid, that we don't have peace, and that we don't have a sound mind. Our self talk is more powerful than the voice of God in our lives sometimes.

In the Word of God, the psalmist often finds himself self-talking. Psalm 10:6 says, "He said in his heart, I will not be moved," and then in Psalm 10:11 the psalmist continues, "He said in his heart, God has forgotten, he hides his face, he will never see it." Psalm 10:13 reiterates his self talk: "He said in his heart, You God will not require yet." The psalmist has found himself in his self-talking. However, too often our self talk leads us *away from* God rather than *toward* Him.

Remember when Adam and Eve sinned and ate the forbidden fruit? The Bible says they were afraid, and instead of Adam's self talk causing him to run toward God, it caused him to run away and hide from God. Have you found this to be a common reaction in your life? When you make mistakes and things haven't worked out right, instead of your self talk warning you to go to church or to turn your heart to God and pray, your self talk tells you just the opposite: "Man, you messed up this time. This is it. God's finished with you. There is no use praying about this one, man. This is a biggie." Self talk.

That's the reason why Paul says in 2 Corinthians 10:5, "We demolish arguments and every pretension that sets up itself against the knowledge of God and we take captive every thought to make it obedient to Christ."

In order to effectively combat self talk, we have to understand where our self talk is taking us. In this book we are going to spend some time looking at the Word of God and the reasons why many of us never enjoy victory or the life God designed for us. We keep up the internal conversations and talk ourselves out of the blessings in life. Paul wrote, "Listen, what you need to do is demolish every argument, every pretense that sets itself against the knowledge of God, and bring it to captivity."

Do you understand that you can be right in your heart with God and yet still wrong in your head? I know people who love God and who have a desire to follow Him. They want to do what God leads them to do, but because they never get their heads right, their self talk keeps taking them down the wrong road...even if their hearts follow after God.

> You can be right in your heart with God and still wrong in your head.

Perhaps you have known a person who has committed multiple sins. Moral failure is the result in such a life, yet that person might say, "I don't know what happened! Why are all these terrible things happening to me?" Recently, someone called my office and said, "Pray for me. I've become an alcoholic." Really? Like alcoholism just shows up? "I've become an alcoholic." Are you kidding me? You had no control over the problem? It is this repeated series of choices and actions that leads to the outcome of a diseased mind and heart. And choices and actions are the result of a series of repeated thoughts. Trace the thought line and trace the actions, and behavior that led down the path to alcoholism can be traced from there.

Could it be true that someone became an alcoholic against his own free will? No, of course not! That's the reason why God's Word says that we have to bring every thought into captivity, every thought that exalts itself against the knowledge of God. Remember what Paul said in Philippians 4:8. We should think about things that are trusted and true and honest and of good report. Dwell on these things in our hearts and in our lives.

Many biblical examples illustrate these internal conversations. One example is in 1 Samuel 30. David is in dire straits. He is in Ziklag, but he leaves suddenly, taking his men to war against the Philistines. When David returns to Ziklag, he discovers that the enemy has captured all of the women and children. In addition, the Philistines have stolen all of their possessions. David's army gets ticked! They weren't used to experiencing defeat of this magnitude. The Bible says that the people thought about killing David.

It's human nature, when things aren't going right, that we want to get rid of the leader because we think it is his fault. "Got to be the boss's fault because he was in charge." But notice in 1 Samuel 30:6, the Bible says David was greatly distressed by the people's talk of stoning him because the souls of his people were grieved. The people grieved for their sons, their daughters, and their husbands and wives, but David encouraged himself in the Lord his God. He self talked! David encouraged himself with a pep talk. He said, "Wait a minute. These guys are against me, but God is for me. The enemy might have come in and stolen from us, but God can help us to take back everything they stole." David gave himself a talk. He poured his life out to God. Through talking about what was going on, he was able to strengthen himself in the Lord his God. David's self talk positively affected him.

Another biblical example of self talk is in Exodus 3. God comes to Moses after the nation of Israel had been in bondage for 400 years in Egypt. The conversation between God and Moses went like this:

> God: I'm going to deliver My people.
> Moses: That's great!
> God: Moses, I'm going to use you.
> Moses: God, You can't use me. I can't even talk plainly. I'm
> slow of speech. Look for somebody else.

Moses's self talk almost robbed him of being one of the greatest instruments that God would use in delivering the nation of Israel.

Some of you know what it is for God to step into your prayer time or into your service and challenge your heart. Perhaps you have heard Him say, "I want to use you. I want you to do this." Your response might be, "God, You don't know me. You don't know my past." Hello, self talk! God understands that sometimes the most powerful voice in the universe is our own self talk. It's often stronger than even God's voice.

When we begin to think negative thoughts and say destructive things to ourselves, we must spring into action. Demolishing and taking those thoughts captive is the first step towards success because the most powerful voice in the universe to any one person is his or her own self talk.

9

ACTION POINTS

1. Can you identify a time when you knew you were right with God in your heart, but your thinking was wrong?

2. Has there ever been a time when you talked yourself out of doing something, even though in your heart you knew you had the gifts or talents to accomplish the task?

3. What steps will you take today to keep your negative thoughts captive?

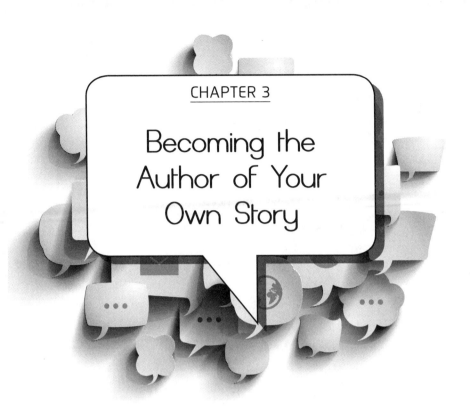

CHAPTER 3

Becoming the Author of Your Own Story

ERE IS THE second principle I want you to get:

It is impossible to walk in constant victory, peace, and joy without gaining victory in the area of our self talk.

Again, that's the reason Paul said we have to bring into captivity every thought that exalts itself against the knowledge of God. Why? It's impossible to live this constant victory of peace and joy without first gaining victory over ourselves.

God understands that our self talk is different from our thought life. Thoughts will come and go—remember, you think at the rate of 1,300 words every minute. But we don't respond to every thought that we have. Just because we might think about slapping somebody, doesn't mean we do it, right? We don't act on every thought we have.

Even though many of our ingrained and persistent thoughts *will* become actions, self talk is stronger even than our active thoughts. This is the reason why it's impossible for us to gain victory in our lives and have the peace and joy God desires for us. We must first gain self victory. And herein lies the power of self talk.

Let me give you another illustration from 1 Samuel 27:1. The Bible says that David thought to himself, "One of these days I will be destroyed by the hand of Saul. Best thing I can do is to escape to the land of the Philistines." We know the Philistines weren't David's friends, but he said, "Saul will give up searching for me anywhere in Israel, and I will slip out of his hands." David's self talk caused him to do one of the most unwise and foolish things he had ever done.

In a weakened condition and being overly tired, perhaps because of Saul's incessant pursuit of him, David did what many of us do. Physical and mental exhaustion caused him to make a disastrous choice. Distressed, David's sharp and godly mind began to engage in negative thoughts. He took his army to the land of the Philistines, but when he arrived there he became totally embarrassed. It takes him a very long time to recover the confidence of his men. David said, "One of these days I will be destroyed by the hand of Saul."

Question: Does the enemy make you say, "One of these days I'm probably going to have heart trouble"? Or does the enemy prompt you to think, "If I don't have a heart attack, maybe I'll have Alzheimer's or maybe I'll end up with high blood pressure"? It's your own self talk at work.

David did not understand that his self talk was go
him to do something very harmful and negative in h
of us can become discouraged or depressed sometimes. ᴗut, like
David, we have other choices that can ensure a different outcome.
David could have gone to his good friend Joab. He could have
approached some of his loyal warriors and said, "Hey, guys, I'm
battling these thoughts about Saul, and I'm thinking that one
of these days he is going to kill me. I'm getting concerned and
fearful." Fear will push you to fight, or fear will push you to
flight. David could have said, "Hey, guys, would you help me
here? Would you stay beside me and keep me from doing something stupid?"

The enemy will start to work in our self talks. The enemy
gloats when our self talks sound like this, "You are not going
to make it this year. Things are going to go badly for you, your
body is going to get sick, and your kids are going to go wrong."
This is when we need to obey God and bring our thoughts
into captivity. Again, it's impossible for you and me to walk in
constant victory without gaining victory over our self talk.

Our third principle:

It has been noted that much of our self talk, if not most of
our thinking, is verbalized.

Behavior research tells us that 77 percent of the thoughts we
have are going to be negative and counterproductive. They are
going to be words that work against us. *Seventy-seven percent of
them!*

> It is impossible to walk in constant victory, peace, and joy without gaining victory in the area of our self talk.

Do you know that repetition is a convincing argument? Again, repetition is a convincing argument! If you are a parent, your kids might say, "Mom, can I go to the store?" No. "Mama, can I go store?" No. "Mommy, can I go to store?" NO. "Mama, can I go to..." And after a while Mom responds, "Go to the store!" Keep these two points in mind: repetition is a convincing argument, and studies have shown that much of our thinking gets verbalized.

Throughout the Scriptures you'll read the phrase, "And he said to himself." Look at this in Genesis 17. God speaks to Abram about changing his name to Abraham. God also talks to Abraham about circumcision and about the covenant. Then He looks at Abraham and says, "Abraham, no longer will your wife be called Sarai, which means princess, but she is going to be called Sarah, meaning 'mother of nations.' And I am going to give you children." The Bible continues in Genesis 17:17, "And Abraham fell face down." (Meaning, "He laughed to himself.")

Abraham fell face down, laughed, and said to himself, "Will a son be born to a man one hundred years old? And will Sarah, the 'mother of nations,' bear a child at the age of ninety? Are you kidding me?" Yes, that's what Abraham was saying! God knows that our self talk is the most powerful voice in the universe. Sadly, it is even more powerful than His own. It was to Abraham. So God kept talking to Abraham, and Abraham kept talking to God, and God won. Sarah eventually had the child Isaac.

In Psalm 10:11 the Bible says, "The wicked man says to himself, God has forgotten and He covers His face and never sees again." Here is a prime example of how the wicked self talk. Some people can keep living an ungodly life even if God keeps extending grace after grace after grace in their lives every day. Basically, the wicked man is saying to himself, "There is no God." The good news is God *does* see, God *doesn't* forget, and He *doesn't* cover His face!

In the New Testament, Jesus said in Matthew 24:48–49, "But suppose that servant is wicked and says to himself, 'My master is staying away a long time,' and he then begins to beat his fellow servants and to eat and drink with drunkards."

Many times the Scripture repeats the fact that we often verbalize our thinking. Our self talk is more than just some trivial thing that we do. Our self talk can affect our destiny. *What you say to yourself can affect your destiny.*

Our fourth principle:

> **There is clear exhortation in Scripture that we are to work on our self talk.** Deuteronomy 9:4 says, "...*do not say to yourself* the Lord has brought me here to take possession of this land because of my righteousness."

In this verse God commands the people of Israel that when they get down to the Promised Land, when they start inheriting what He has given them, when they start possessing what

He desires, they should not say to themselves that it happened because of their own righteousness.

Do you know how to keep blessings flowing in your life? Do you know how to keep God's favor upon you? By remembering every day that your blessings are because of God's favor in your life. Not because you are such a smart humdinger! "I've worked hard, and I have all this stuff. Look at what I have, look at my car, look at this..." No, the only reason you have anything is because of God's favor in your life, not because of yourself.

Our thoughts should be focused on God's provision and care. They should be fixed on the words of God. Our thoughts should be about what God says. Deuteronomy 11:18–19 says, "Therefore you shall lay up these words of mine in your heart and in your soul, and bind them as a sign on your hand, and they shall be as frontlets between your eyes. You shall teach them to your children, speaking of them when you sit in your house, when you walk by the way, when you lie down, and when you rise up." When you lie down, where are your thoughts?

Our lives and our circumstances should always be God-centered. Say to yourself, "God supplies all my needs according to His riches and glory," not "How am I going to pay for this bill?" These commands and others constantly tell us to see life from God's perspective. We are commanded to do this.

The encouraging thing is that if God commands us to do something, He also gives us the ability to do it. He is not going to frustrate us by saying, "I want you to have positive self talk. I don't want you to think that it's all about you. I don't want you to dwell on the problem." If He tells us to do it, He will give us the power to follow through.

In our society many will argue that virtually any behavior,

thought, or pattern can be altered by the messages we tell ourselves. Solomon said this in Proverbs 23:7: "As a man thinks in his heart, so is he." Some would react with emotion to Solomon's statement. They might say, "I am what I *think*, really?" That's what Solomon says. The Bible affirms that our thinking is often verbalized. Undoubtedly, there are definite benefits to thinking positive thoughts, but, lest you misunderstand, this is not a self-help book. This book will focus on the Word of God, but there are definite benefits to having positive thoughts.

Husbands, you know your day is going to be difficult if you get up in the morning, look at your wife, and say, "Wow, you look horrible!" Your day is going to be considerably better if you wake up, look at your wife, and say, "You are beautiful. I love you so much." Likewise, do you think if you spent thirty minutes every morning getting ready for work, while cursing your job the entire time, that you will be able to walk in the doors of your workplace and have a great day? But what if you get up and say, "God, thank you for giving me a job to support my family. Thank you for the blessing of my job"? Which morning routine do you think is going to cause you to have a better day? No doubt about it. Positive thought works. But there is more than just positive thinking involved in the problem of self talk.

The Bible stops short of any notion that self talk is the key to our problems. It stops short of saying we need to think positive. Positive thinking in itself is often just glorified, wishful thinking. God is not in the wishful thinking business. For example, you get up in the morning, you look at yourself in the mirror, and you say, "You are 6'2" and handsome." But if you are 5'2" and average looking, self talking isn't going to help. Self talk isn't an instant guarantee to health, happiness, and wealth.

There is an old cartoon strip called *Archie and Jughead*. Jughead has a task that he needs to do, and he doesn't feel like he can do it. He feels like he is not qualified. Archie looks at him and says, "Jughead, just think positive and tell yourself you are going to succeed," to which Jughead replies, "That won't work!" When Archie asks him why, Jughead replies, "Because I know what a liar I am!"

Some of us know what liars we are, so thinking positive thoughts or giving ourselves positive self-affirmation is not going to be the cure-all. God understands this.

That brings me to the fifth principle, perhaps, the most important point:

What happens TO me is often out of my realm of responsibility, but what happens IN me is completely within my control.

What happens *in* me has much more to do with the story that I tell myself than what happens *to* me. Sometimes, what happens to us is totally out of our control and responsibility. The most powerful effects are caused by what we tell ourselves constantly about those events. It's what you tell yourself that matters. There is power in the story you rehearse in your mind.

In summary:

A. Something happens to me.
B. I begin to constantly and persistently talk to myself about what happened.
C. This begins forming my personality, my character, and my view of life in general.

We have all been hurt. The pain of an offense may come from family and childhood experiences, people outside the family, life, or even from ourselves. Some people may even be offended by God and blame Him for painful experiences. Self talk about the painful event may become so persistent and ingrained that we cannot release ourselves to move forward from it.

In Genesis 35, Jacob and his wife Rachel were leaving Bethel and going to Ephrath when Rachel went into labor. At the heighth of her labor pains, the midwife said, "Don't worry, Rachel. You are going to have another boy." Some women might respond to this comment in their pain, "Who cares? Don't speak to me!" When my wife was giving birth to our second child, I was coaching and helping her by quoting Scripture. During one of her severe labor pains, she grabbed my tie, pulled me down toward her face, and said, "If you quote one more Bible verse to me, I'm going to hit you." I was just trying to help her with "I can do all things through Jesus Christ who..." But her response was unequivocal: "Get out of my face."

Rachel's birth bed became her death bed. The Bible tells us that, as she lay dying, she named her son Benoni, meaning "son of my pain." Benoni would forever carry the curse that he was the son of his mother's pain. With this name, Rachel would remind her son daily that he lived and she died. That's a huge weight to put on a baby. Yes, hurting people hurt people. Jacob spoke up and said, "His name will not be Benoni. His name will be Benjamin, meaning 'son of good fortune'." Although what happens to me may be out of my control, I must constantly remind myself that those events will form my personality, my character, and my view of life.

Often children will inherit the pain of their parents. Rachel tried to put her pain upon Benjamin. "I want you to be known as the son of my pain," she said, and Jacob responded, "Not on my life." One of the most important things you can do for a child is to make sure they know how blessed and favored of God they are. Remind them daily that God has a plan and a purpose for their lives, and He is going to do something miraculous with them. Children need this positive reinforcement.

What we hear from other people can feed our self-talk problem. Someone's offending words to us can replay over and over in our minds like a broken record. If we verbalize the pain of our self talk, it can offend those around us. For instance, if a divorced parent constantly tells everyone in earshot about the sins of the other person or the trials of raising children alone, imagine the effect on the children's self-esteem to have these issues continually rehearsed before them.

Second Samuel 13 gives us a biblical example. David had two sons, Amnon and Absalom, and a daughter named Tamar. Amnon lusted after his sister and developed a plan to get Tamar alone and try to lay with her. Tamar rejected Amnon and fought him off, but he raped her. David didn't do anything about this offense. He completely ignored it, but Absalom, David's other son, never got over this insult to his sister. For two years Absalom plotted how he would kill Amnon. For two years the bitterness engendered by the rape of Tamar stayed inside his spirit until finally he killed his brother, Amnon.

Absalom might have been reminded, "It's not what happens to me or those I love, but it's the story that I tell myself." Absalom did not understand why David failed to respond. Perhaps David felt guilty because his many wives, children, and responsibilities of state gave him little time to be a true father to his children. He dealt with the guilt by being soft and indulgent with his children. Parents are not perfect. As hard as they try and as much as they want to, parents don't always make the right decisions.

Absalom refused to understand this about his father David, so in two years Amnon was dead. David lost a daughter and a son, and although he longed to see Absalom, he waited three more years before even trying to have a conversation with him. By then it was too late. Bitterness had set like concrete in Absalom's life. He set his mind to rip the kingdom away from David. A concert of rivalry began between Absalom and his father that ended with Absalom's death.

Like Absalom, many people today are daily strangling themselves on things that happened to them over which they had no control. They may have had no responsibility for what happened *to* them, but they do have responsibility and control for what is happening *in* them. The litany, "I'll never get a break. Life has never been fair to me," can destroy lives. It is negative, destructive self talk.

You have got to constantly ask yourself, "Where is my MAP? Where is my Mindset, my Attitude, my Priority?" Proverbs 19:11 reminds us, "A man's wisdom gives him patience; it is to his glory to overlook an offense." If it is to your glory to overlook an offense, then take responsibility for what happens *in* you. You are the architect of your thought life. Determine to be the author of a successful thought life and the author of your story. Let God teach you to say, "It is well with my soul."

If we decide to be the author of our own thought lives, we will know our MAP, our mindset, attitude, and priority. We will ask ourselves, "Is this true? Is it helpful? Is it honest? Is it of good report?" Remember, what you believe about yourself and what you believe about God are not linked as closely to what happened *to* you as to what happens *in* you right now. Where are your mindset, your attitude, and your priority taking you?

Solomon said, "As a man thinks in his heart so is he." In other words, we must be the gatekeepers of our thoughts because gatekeepers can overcome negative self talk. Not all of our thoughts are self talk, but many of them will be, and 77 percent of them are going to be negatives. So I have to decide if I will be the gate-keeper of my mind. Will I watch out for right motives and attitudes? Will I monitor the soundtrack playing in my ear today? What is my mental iPod telling me? Is it condemning or encouraging me? Do I hear the tune, "I'm hopeless! I'm stupid! Nobody loves me!"? What are the lyrics you are listening to? How do you feel about the contents of your "thought closet"? Whatever thoughts we hang in that closet will be the clothing of our minds. Our mindset, attitude, and priorities strongly influence us. We must learn to govern them with truthful self talk.

ACTION POINTS

1. King David thought his future was more negative than positive. In what ways can you identify with David?

2. If all of your self conversations were recorded and played back to you at the end of the day, what percentage would be negative and what percentage would be positive?

3. Where is your MAP (mindset, attitude, priority) taking you?

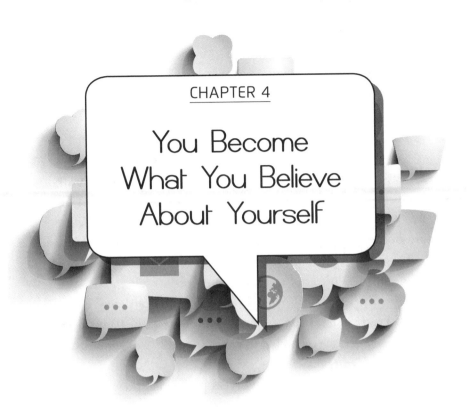

CHAPTER 4

You Become What You Believe About Yourself

HAVE YOU EVER met someone who considers every disaster, problem, or situation a spiritual event? Sometimes these issues are simply about making the right choices and being accountable for our success. It is an error to think every problem is a spiritual problem and requires a spiritual answer.

A great example of this is in 1 Kings 18–19. Elijah has been in conflict with Baal, Jezebel, her 400 followers, and the 450 prophets. He claimed victory for God when fire came down from heaven. Elijah had all 850 of them killed. Jezebel, as you can imagine, did not take this well. She sent Elijah a letter and said, "I'm going to kill you." Elijah panicked. He ran in fear into the wilderness where he sat under a tree and said, "I just want to die. I just want to die." When he fell asleep, an angel woke him and told him to eat. Elijah found a cake and some water beside him, and he ate and drank before he fell asleep again.

The angel woke him a second time and told him, "You'd better eat, or you won't have the energy to make the journey you're about to take." Elijah awoke and ate again. Then he headed off to Horeb, also known as Sinai, the mountain of God. During his journey of forty days and forty nights, he didn't eat anything.

Often when problems occur, we think the answer is spiritual. Sometimes there is not a spiritual answer to what you need to do initially. God knew what Elijah needed. God knew Elijah needed rest, and he needed nourishment because he hadn't been sleeping or eating very well. When we are tired, our self talk can definitely take us down the wrong path.

Sometimes people think that every problem in their marriage is spiritual. Someone might say, "I've got to pray. The devil has really come against my marriage." Really, is it the devil? Or is it just your self talk? If you are always putting your spouse down and saying demeaning things to them or to your children, and problems arise because of this abuse, do you really think it's spiritual? It's not spiritual, You've just got to get rid of your "stinkin' thinkin'." Your spouse and your children are gifts from God and should be treated like the gifts they are. Watch your problems fall away when you do!

You can fast all you want to fast. You can pray all you want to pray, but if your thinking doesn't change, and your words don't change, the situation isn't going to get better. It's going to get worse.

> It is an error to think every problem is a spiritual problem and always has a spiritual answer.

God knew Elijah needed to relax. He reminded Elijah, "I've got everything under control." When things are going awry in your life, you need to do a quick search and realize, "I haven't sinned or willfully walked away from God's promises. I haven't done anything, so what do I have to do? I've just got to stay focused."

We must be especially watchful for harmful self talk when we feel alone, isolated, and fearful. These are the times when we get into trouble. That was the place where Elijah found himself. When we are isolated, alone, and fearful, our self talk can become deadly. God knew that Elijah needed rest and nourishment even though his mind was filled with death.

We cannot give what we do not have. Some people may think it is selfish to help themselves before they help others, but we have to look in the mirror before we can look out the window. Remember the first person we lead in life is ourselves. You have heard the instructions given to passengers on an airplane: "If you are traveling with small children, place the oxygen mask on yourself first, then on the child." We cannot give to others what we do not have ourselves! In Acts 3:6 Peter said, "Silver or gold I do not have, but what I *have* I give you..."

Truthfully, there are no quick fixes for negative, destructive self talk. The Scriptures never come close to suggesting that our lives will be dramatically and eternally changed by eliminating it completely. Nor do the Scriptures suggest that those ingrained habits of destructive thinking can be quickly changed merely by focusing on our self talk alone. While the Bible is highly optimistic about positive change occurring in our lives, it cautions us against any attempt at a quick fix.

This is illustrated vividly in a discussion that Jesus had with His disciples about faith. On one occasion in Luke 17:5, they came to Him with an understandable request: "Increase our faith!" Perhaps they were envious of Jesus's remarkable thought control abilities. They wanted His uncanny capacity to believe without wavering that they could heal someone, or that needs in their own lives would be instantly met. They wanted to get rid of all those negative messages inside their heads that kept saying, "This is impossible." Instead, Jesus replied, "If you have faith as small as a mustard seed, you can say to this mulberry tree, 'Be uprooted and planted by the sea,' and it will obey you" (Luke 17:6).

At first His reply seems puzzling, for He had only spoken to them about the challenge of increasing their faith, not about *how* to do it. He didn't seem to answer the question they asked. Jesus realized His disciples were looking for an easy shortcut to faith. Jesus gives them a reality check. He jolted them into acknowledging the extreme difficulty of what they were asking, for it was in *their* choices and *their* free will that the level of their faith was determined.

Most of us know that it takes more than a few efforts at thought control, or the wave of a spiritual magic wand, to bring about an authentic change in outlook. It requires nothing less than a true inner transformation. Such a transformation requires God's power and His process working in us.

This point is vitally important to our discussion of self talk because our concern for improving our self talk is, after all, a need to increase our faith. So Jesus reminds us that our greatest faith need is not to experience a *complete* change in perspective. It's about becoming *thoroughly persuaded* of Christ's vibrant outlook on our lives, not just temporarily enthused about it.

Here are two action points:

1. Simply ask for the Holy Spirit's help to edit the story that you constantly tell yourself. What is the story that you are telling yourself about any event or any circumstance that has happened in your life? Is it true? Is it honest? Is it of good report? Is it taking you in the right direction? Or is that story constantly pulling you down? Ask the Holy Spirit to give you help to edit that story. Some of you have had some horrible things happen to you. I'm not going to belittle that. I cannot belittle your dismissal from a job, or your divorce, or your abuse. I am simply saying that today you can make the choice to allow the Holy Spirit to give you the power to start editing your story in your mind. God's Spirit can give you the power to take captive every thought that brings itself against the knowledge of God.

2. Take the responsibility to be the gatekeeper of your own thoughts and your own self talk. Be the gatekeeper to guard what you are thinking—guard what's coming in and what's going out. Jeremiah 31:3 reminds us that the Lord said, "Yes, I have loved you with an everlasting love; therefore with loving kindness I have drawn you." Someone reading this may need to know that God says, "I have loved you with everlasting love." Refuse to believe the lies of Satan. Last year might have been a difficult year. It might have been a struggle physically, emotionally, financially, and relationally, but God still says, "I have loved you with everlasting love, and I have drawn you with loving kindness." God is for you, not against you. He wants you to stop repeating lies about yourself. He wants you to be assured that you are fearfully and wonderfully made.

So are you ready for God to turn this year around for you? Stop shooting yourself in the foot with your words. Change your core thinking habits. Don't come to Him thinking that He is just one more additive. Jesus has to be the number one source in your life. He has to be the Lord, the King, and the lead love of your life. If you've never asked Him into your life, if you've never surrendered and said, "God, without You I am lost! I love You, Jesus!" then today let me challenge you to tell Him, "God, I want to be in Your family."

ACTION POINTS

1. Has the statement "Every problem is a spiritual problem and has a spiritual answer" ever caused you to doubt your relationship with Christ or your spiritual maturity?

2. What steps will you take to begin the "editing process" of how you remember the events you have encountered in your life?

3. How will you commit to the process of changing your thoughts in order to change your life?

CHAPTER 5

The Difference Between Talking to Yourself and Letting Yourself Talk to You

HAVE YOU EVER wondered why some people can be so confident and resilient while others seem to be struggling with anxieties, fear, discouragement, and depression? One of the things that we know from the Bible, as well as from human nature, is that many times these varied reactions to life circumstances have to do with self talk.

Self talk can influence your mood, behavior, and your response to life. Self talk is universal—everyone does it, even though we may not like to admit it. It's acceptable to be self-aware but not to be continually self-critical. Recognize the power of self talk in your life and change it.

Some studies show that the average American has about

thirty conversations a day. About one-fifth of our entire life is spent talking. For some people it may be less than that; for others it is considerably more. Statistics tell us that men talk about 20,000 words a day, and women talk about 30,000 words a day. In has been said that one year of conversations has enough words in it to fill sixty-six books with 800 pages each.

You may have heard it said that a person might be born with a "silver foot in his mouth." Some of us have the natural tendency to say exactly the wrong thing at the wrong time. Have you ever found yourself guilty of this dreaded foot-in-mouth disease?

A young produce clerk in a grocery store had this problem. One day a lady approached him and said, "I'd like to buy a half a head of lettuce." The clerk went to ask his manager if this would be possible. He laughed, "Sir, you're not going to believe this. There's this stupid old lady out there. She wants to buy a half a head of lettuce." Looking over his shoulder, he realized that she had followed him. Very quickly he continued, "And this fine lady right here would like to buy the other half. Is that okay?"

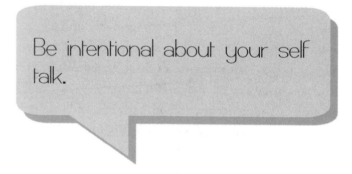

Be intentional about your self talk.

Self talk has the potential and power to make or break a person. Some might say, "God is all-powerful." But many of us could also attest to the fact that there have been times in our lives when our voices drowned out God's.

Fear is a strong factor in amplifying our voice over God's. God says in 2 Timothy 3:5, "I've not given you the spirit of fear, but power, love, and sound mind." God wants us to know that He did not give us that fear. We take on that fear, we nurse it, and we hold on to it. More powerful than the voice of any person, more powerful even than the voice of God, is the voice you speak to yourself. What we have to do is what Paul says in 2 Corinthians 10:5: "We demolish arguments and every pretense that sets itself up against the knowledge of God, and we take captive every thought to make it obedient to Christ."

Paul admonishes us to be aware of what's going on inside our thoughts. It will take focus, fortitude, and tenacity to demolish those arguments that war against us. Those things that are false in our minds begin to exalt themselves against the knowledge of God. Only through the power of Jesus Christ can we bring everything under submission to Him.

> Self talk can influence your mood, behavior, and response toward life.

Another source of wrong patterns of self talk develops in childhood. It has been noted that a child growing up in an average, reasonably positive home will have heard over 148,000 repetitions of the phrase, "No, you can't do that" by the time they reach the age of eighteen. Did you know that two-year-olds hear the word "no" 77 percent of their waking hours? It is no wonder that "no" is one of the first words that a two-year-old learns to say. A four-year-old or three-year-old will hear the word "no" some 400 times a day. "No, don't do that. No, don't you...No, you can't...no, no, no, no." Such negativity in the environment can program our minds and write a script that will plot our lives. As a result, we begin to say to ourselves, "I can't do that," or "I will never be able to do..." or "I am so stupid."

With time we begin to believe what we've been told, and we add our two cents' worth to the problem. Why is that? Because, eventually, we become what we most believe about ourselves. Repetition is a pretty convincing argument. If you hear something long enough, if it's ingrained in you over and over, it will likely become your truth. Life scripts are etched by attacks like, "You are stupid. You're lazy. You're good for nothing. You're just like your dad." Layer by layer our self images are created, and in time our minds join the chant. We begin to say, "I can't do that" or "I've never been good at that" or "I always mess up." **In time we become what we most believe about ourselves.**

Paul said that when we come to Christ, our spirits are born again. We are new in Christ. But our *minds* do not become born again. So what has to happen? Even after I come to Christ, *my mind has to be renewed every day, and my body has to be subdued.* We have to learn how to say, "Wait a minute, what is true and what is untrue?" Without evaluating what we think, in time we will become what we believe most about ourselves. So negative thoughts like, "You're good for nothing. You're just a druggie.

You've got an alcohol problem. You have an anger issue. You talk too much," can lead to despair in our lives.

The psalmists offer wonderful testimony for dealing with negative self talk or destructive voices from outside. Psalm 42 is an example of positive responses to discouragement, depression, and despondency:

> As the deer pants for the water brooks, so my soul pants for Thee, O God. My soul thirsts for God, for the living God. When shall I come and appear before God? My tears have been my food day and night, while they say to me all the day long, "Where is your God? These things I remember, as I pour out my soul within me. For I used to go along with the throng and lead them in procession to the house of God with a voice of joy and thanksgiving and a multitude keeping festival. Why are you in despair, O my soul, and why have you become disturbed within me? Hope in God; for I shall again praise him, for the help of his presence. O my God, My soul is in despair within me; therefore I remember the from the land of Jordan and of Hermon, and Mount Mizar. Deep calls to deep at the sound of Thy waterfalls; all Thy breakers and all Thy waves roll over me.
>
> The Lord will command his loving kindness in the daytime and his song will be with me at night, a prayer to the God of my life. I will say to God, my rock: "Why hast thou forgotten me? Why do I go mourning because of the oppression of the enemy?" Has it shattered in my bones, my adversaries revile me, while they say to me all the day long, "Where is your God?" Why are you in despair, O my soul, and why have you come so disturbed within me?

Hope in God; for I shall yet praise him, the Lord and Thy
countenance and my God.

—PSALM 42

The emotional state of David, the presumed author, is
apparent. He fights the highs and lows of his circumstances.
Through endless tears he cries, "Why are you in despair, O my
soul?" His tears prevent him from eating. He remembers earlier
days of joy in the Lord, days when their relationship was close.
But he listened to outside critics, and now David wonders, "Has
God abandoned me?" He concludes, "Why have You forsaken
me?" David's angst is obvious. Like David we can have a heart
after God's own heart, we can have passion for God, and we
can have a desire to go to heaven, but because of our "stinkin'
thinkin'" we find ourselves in anguish.

The critics may see this and attack: "Where's God now?
You've got marriage problems. Where is He in your marriage?
You're dealing with financial issues. Where's this God of blessing
now?" If we listen to the critics, we begin to think, "Why has
God forgotten me?" But notice, *David worked through his strug-
gles by talking to himself about the character of God by reciting
biblical truth.* David reminded himself of God's presence and of
His "loving kindness in the daytime and His song at night."

God created us. He made us, and He understands our
humanity, which causes us to struggle. He understands that we
struggle with negative self talk and destructive outside voices
that say, "Where is God?" God responds to us, "Remember,
who I am." David says, "Hope in God." We can also be confident in God, His faithfulness, His presence, and His love.

ACTION POINTS

1. Within the last week, how has self talk influenced your mood, behavior, or response toward life?

2. How has the script that others have given you for your life influenced what you believe about yourself?

3. Considering King David's approach to despondency, what steps can you take today to allow God's Word to help you talk to yourself instead of letting yourself talk to you?

CHAPTER 6

The Voice of Truth

THERE IS A difference between talking to ourselves and letting ourselves talk to us.

Martin Lloyd has a great book entitled *Spiritual Depressions: Its Causes and Its Cures*. In that book he writes, "The main trouble in this whole matter of discouragement and depression, depression is a sense of this that we allow ourselves to talk to us, instead of talking to ourselves."

One of the key factors of our unhappiness in life is that we are listening to ourselves instead of talking to ourselves. David listened to himself.

When you get up in the morning, thoughts come into your mind many times. Those thoughts can bring back the problems of yesterday or our worries about tomorrow. Those thoughts don't originate with you. Sometimes they can be fed to you through listening to the news about the weather of the day. A bad weather report can make you think, "Aw, it's going to be a hard day today. There will be rough traffic. Everybody's going to drive like a jerk."

The daily cycle of letting ourselves talk to us begins. You might say, "This is a brand new day!" Then your mind says, "Yeah, but you still have yesterday's unsolved problems. They didn't go anywhere." Or perhaps you begin to think about the future, and worries about what tomorrow will bring fill your mind when you haven't even made it through today. Have you ever found yourself talking back and forth like that?

What I consistently tell myself about what happens to me is actually more powerful than what does happen to me.

David understood that reciting biblical truth would help him to work through his struggles. He reminded himself of what God is like. David knew what to say to himself, and we should too. A spiritual principle in our lives is to know how to handle ourselves, address ourselves, preach to ourselves, or sometimes question ourselves. Some of us need to sit down and say, "Listen here, self. I want to tell you what God says about this situation."

An example of this negative self talk might relate to your health. Is diabetes or cancer prominent in your family medical history? Do you tell yourself you are going to get it, too? Tell yourself that you are not going to let the fear of the diagnosis control you. Refuse to latch onto those thoughts just because the doctors say it's in the genes. You have new genes! Christ's genes are inside of you. The Great Healer lives inside of us.

David worked through these struggles by talking to himself. When you start stating biblical truth about God, guess what we can do? We can flush out this self focus with the fresh, living water and God's hope. Believe what God says about you. He loves you.

> In time we start becoming what we most believe about ourselves.

Remember, **what happens *to* you is often out of your realm of responsibility, but what happens *in* you is your responsibility.** We're not always responsible for what happens to us. Sometimes things are out of our control. Some say David was writing Psalm 42 when Absalom, his son, was leading a rebellion against him. In the last chapter we discussed Absalom, Amnon, and Tamar, and David's inappropriate response to Tamar's rape. In the midst of the struggle, David could not control what was happening to him. The only thing he could control was what was happening *in* him. David's critics continued to taunt him, "Where is your God?" But David maintained, "I don't know where He is, but my hope is in God alone."

ACTION POINTS

1. Tell about a time when the voice of truth was drowned out in your life by negative self talk.

2. What benefits do we receive by reciting biblical truths to ourselves instead of negative self talk?

3. Describe an event in which you discovered this truth: "What happened to me was out of my realm of responsibility, but what happened in me was my responsibility."

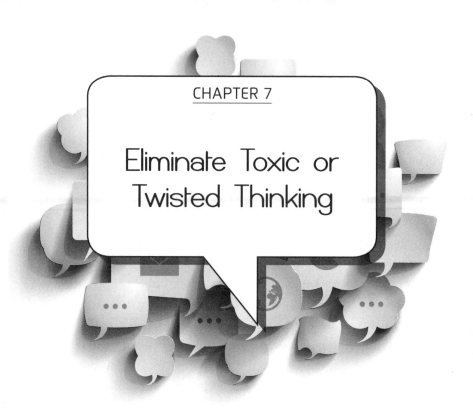

CHAPTER 7

Eliminate Toxic or Twisted Thinking

THE CONCEPT OF surrender means that each and every day we must surrender to God's will and His plan for our lives.

As part of our transformation process, we need to go after three main areas in our walk with God. The first area is our *thought life*. We are what we think. When you and I come to Christ, we are born again. Yes, we're re-created. We are going to heaven when we die. But your mind has to be renewed, also. Every day we must bring our thought lives under subjection to the authority of God's Word. We must ask ourselves, "God, what are You saying to me? I can overcome this. I am a conqueror in Christ Jesus."

The second area of our lives that we should target in this transformation process is our *word life*. Our word life has to do with the words we speak to others. Remember, you may be the only Jesus some people meet. Be aware of the words you leave behind. You never know who is listening!

The third area of focus should be our *action life*, how we're going to behave. Actions most often speak louder than words to those observing us. As Christians, we are held accountable even more for our actions. The world is watching us. Represent Christ well in your actions as well as your words.

Thought life, word life, and action life. These are the areas of my life that must be transformed through the Word of God, my relationship with Jesus Christ, and the power of the Holy Spirit. Each day, submit your thought life to God through a prayer like this: "God, I want to bring my mind under Your subjection. I want to demolish every thought, every pretense, and every thing that is being exalted against You. I want to bring them under Your subjection. God, I want my thoughts to affect what I'm going to say." Remind yourself, "I can do all things through Christ."

Develop the tools that go along with surrender, and be committed to surrendering your life, your mind, your words, and your actions each day to God.

Proverbs 18:21 says, "Death and life are in the power of the tongue." In the New Testament, Jesus said in Matthew 12, "For by your word you're going to be acquitted. By your word you're going to be condemned." Words have power. They can acquit or condemn us. Think of the responsibility and ramifications of this revelation. Our words can either bring life or bring death! We can either choose to learn how to speak and release positive words of love, encouragement, and edification, or we can choose to release negative words of condemnation and criticism. The choice is ours!

We have all felt the joy of being on the receiving end of words that show love, encouragement, and edification. Right words have an incredible power to build our sense of self-esteem, self-worth, and self-confidence. Good words can literally be health to our bones, says the writer of Proverbs 16:24. In other words, good and positive words can produce physical health. As a result, your immune system will receive a boost.

However, just the reverse is also possible. If children only hear stern, abusive words of condemnation, criticism, and negativity from their parents as they are growing up, their self-esteem and self-worth can be severely affected. Sooner or later, the child will end up believing the lies of his parents, and he will grow up thinking that he will never be good enough and will never amount to anything worthwhile.

There are many adults who never accomplish anything that God had in store for them in this life because they were not able to pull out of the negativity and pessimism that their parents heaped on them during their growing years. In addition, their growth in the Lord is stunted as a result of the negativity of their parents and later by their own self talk. Our thoughts and self talk strongly influence us so we must learn to govern them with truthful self talk.

Consider these questions:

How different would your life be if . . .

1. Your relationships had been different?
2. Your beliefs had been different?
3. Your thoughts had been different?
4. Your values had been different?
5. Your words had been different?

Some of us talk ourselves out of God's blessings before He ever gets a chance to do anything. I've seen it in church over the years when we have altar calls. During the sermon people sense God speaking to them, but in the journey from their seat to the front of the church, they give in to themselves and the critics they have heard over the years who said, "You'll never get loose from this. You'll never get out of this habit. You'll never be free from this hurdle. You're always going to have this hanging over you."

Much of this self talk begins when we are children. I can play piano. I don't claim to be a master, but I can also play almost any instrument that has strings. I can play guitar, banjo, mandolin, bass fiddle, and organ. Do you know where I got the confidence to do that? When I was five or six years old, I remember hearing my daddy say, "Phillip can play anything. I mean, if it's got strings on it, he can play it." I was just unintelligent enough to believe him. I didn't know any better. Dad's comment gave me confidence. At churches and revivals, I would sneak my way to the platform and start playing.

> Every day we have to bring our thought life under subjection to the authority of God's Word.

I couldn't play chords when I first started, and I wasn't always in the same key or on the same chord as the band, but I can remember Mom and Dad saying, "He can play anything." I never sat down to play any instrument and felt intimidated. I was going to find a way to play it.

I had been playing the banjo and guitar, but one day I said to my father, "Dad, I want to play a mandolin." He said, "Save up your money, buy one, and see what you can do with it." I saved my money, and I purchased it. I bought all of my instruments. We lived in a little trailer park in Alabama, and when my mandolin came in, I went out back, found a little tree, sat down, and taught myself my first song: "My Bonnie lies over the ocean. My Bonnie lies over the sea. O bring back my Bonnie to me." I played it about an hour. When I got home, I said, "Dad, I want to play my mandolin in church this weekend." He said, "Can you play it?" I said, "Well, I can play 'My Bonnie Lies Over the Ocean'. I think I can get 'I'll Fly Away.'"

Parents, your words have life or death. We can acquit our kids and ourselves with our words, or we can condemn them.

ACTION POINTS

1. Can you identify some ways that your thoughts, words, and actions help or hurt you in your walk with Christ?

2. What can you do with past pains so they will be rewritten as battles won and not scars collected?

3. How can you ensure that your words will be filled with life and not death toward others?

CHAPTER 8

Identifying Your Big Five

Wゃ HAT'S STANDING IN the way of success in your life?
What are the roadblocks to this surrender to life
transformation? Identify them and eliminate them.
Focus on God's plan.

The Bible says in Proverbs 16:24, "Pleasant words are as a
honeycomb, sweet to the soul, and health to the bones." They are
health to our marrow; they are health to our immune system.
You know how good it makes you feel when someone says,
"Don't you look nice today!" You think, "I do look good! I feel
pretty good, too." And you also know the effect on your mind
when someone says, "Are you okay? Your complexion just isn't
right." Before you realize it, you wonder *Do I really feel great? I*

think I'm feeling ill. Have you ever experienced this? Have you ever let somebody lead you down the road to self-doubt?

God says we have to learn how to talk to ourselves rather than letting ourselves talk to us. Good and positive words will give you better health, and your immune system will receive a boost. However, just the reverse is also possible. We have already discussed the negative impact on children of abusive words or condemnation and criticism. Bombardments of negativity from co-workers, friends, and family will affect our self talk. That's why David asked God to set a guard over his mouth. Setting that guard on our mouths and keeping watch over our words are vital because the most powerful voice in this universe is your own self talk.

Mark 5 tells a story of a woman's faith. A woman, who had suffered a hemorrhaging condition for twelve years, visited a long succession of physicians, but they treated her badly, taking all of her money and leaving her worse off than before. She heard about Jesus. She slipped into the crowd behind Jesus and touched His robe. She thought to herself, "If I can put a finger on His robe, I can get well." The Bible says this woman had been anemic for twelve years. She was in pitiful condition, and her misery was compounded by the fact that she was financially bereft and probably very disgusted and depressed. The moment she touched Jesus's robe, the flow of blood dried up. She could feel the change and knew the plague was over.

This woman's self talk caused her faith to be strong, tenacious, and determined. Even though she was in a weakened condition, the Bible says that she pushed through the throng of crowds and past many people to lay hold of the garment of Jesus. This miracle happened because the woman heard of Jesus, and she repeated her reason for hope to herself. Matthew 9:21 says it like this: "She kept saying to herself." Through self talk she confronted her fears and doubts. By telling herself repeatedly that she had a reason for hope, her past no longer had a grip on her. Her past did not have to define her future.

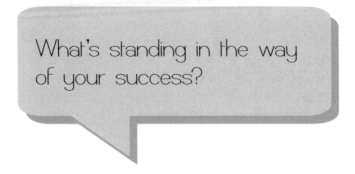

What's standing in the way of your success?

Our self talk has the ability to fill us with faith or doubt, generosity or greed, courage or fear, confidence or insecurity. What if this woman had heard about Jesus and said, "It's too late. I don't have anything now. I'm broke. I'm weaker than I was before. I'm glad Jesus, is healing people, but it's too late for me. It won't work for me. I'd never be able to meet Jesus"? But she didn't say that. She heard about Jesus and her self talk convinced and encouraged her that it might be possible for her to be healed.

The most important self conversation we have every day should be about Jesus. When we start talking about Jesus, when we start telling people what Jesus is doing, when we start lifting up Jesus and His power, when we start exalting Jesus, get ready. God's going to do something in our lives.

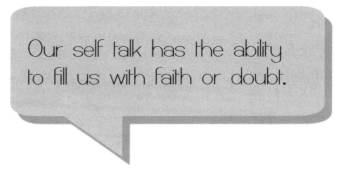

Our self talk has the ability to fill us with faith or doubt.

By aligning our thinking with God and His Word, we can change our self talk. So how do we align our thinking with God and His Word? Paul says in Romans 12:2 that we should realize that we can't do life on our own and allow Him to help us. Take your everyday ordinary life, your sleeping, eating, working, and walking through life, and place it before God as an offering. Embracing what God does for you is the best thing you can do for Him. He said we shouldn't become so well adjusted to our culture that we fit into it without even thinking. Instead, our attention should be fixed on God. You'll be changed from the inside out. Readily recognize what He wants from you, quickly respond to it, and unlock the culture around you that is always dragging you down to its level, a level of immaturity. God brings the best out of you and develops well-formed maturity in you. We do this by aligning ourselves with God's Word. Remember: if we get our thinking into alignment with God and His Word, we can change our self talk.

Every day here's what we need to do to align ourselves with God. Bring the Big Five to God every day. Bring your motives, attitudes, thoughts, words, and actions into alignment with God and His Word. Using the example of the ill woman in Mark 5, we should say to ourselves:

Motive: I don't *want* to live like this.

Attitude: I don't *have* to live like this.

Thoughts: I *won't* live like this.

Words: If I touch Jesus, I will be healed.

Action: She did it.

What was this woman's motive for getting to Jesus? Her motive was simply, "I don't want to live like this." That's the only motive you need sometimes. "I don't want to." Her attitude was, "I don't have to live like this." And her words were, "If I touch Him, I'll be healed." Her action was...she did it.

Every day I bring my motives, my attitudes, my thoughts, my words, and my actions into alignment with God's Word. Do this with your life. Bring your hurts, habits, and hang-ups. Bring your relationships, your fears, and your doubts. Bring all of this and line it up with God's Word. Joshua said it like this in Joshua 1:8: "Keep this book of law always on your lips. Meditate on it day and night so that you'll be careful to do everything written in it. Then you will be prosperous and successful."

ACTION POINTS

1. Can you identify a motive, attitude, thought, word, or action that is currently keeping you from success?

2. Does your self talk fill your life with faith or doubt?

3. How will you allow your Big Five to work for you and not against you?

CHAPTER 9

You Don't Grow What You Don't Sow

W HAT ACTION ARE you taking each day to change your self talk? How are you investing in your life by changing your self talk? The only resource for victory in our minds is offered through biblical truth. This is where we will find help for our self talk.

One way to gain biblical truth is by meditating on God's Word. When the Bible talks about meditating on the Word, it doesn't mean some type of incantations or some lotus posture. When God mentions meditating on His Word, He doesn't mean chanting "omm" and emptying our minds to reach nirvana. That's mysticism.

Meditating on the Word of God simply means bringing our

thoughts, motives, attitudes, words, and actions to God. Meditating means we quietly ponder, think about, or reflect on what God has done through His Son, Jesus Christ. We monitor our thoughts because our thoughts can become our words, our words become our actions, our actions become our habits, our habits become our characters, and our character becomes our destiny.

The woman with the hemorrhaging condition, mentioned in Mark 5 and discussed in the last chapter had an extraordinary faith. Her faith did not come from psyching herself up. She didn't tell herself, "I can do this, I can do this, I can do this." No, it wasn't about psyching herself up. She had a deep conviction inside of her about God's grace and goodness. She *heard* about Jesus. That strong, deep conviction so persuaded her, so convinced her, that she spoke to her *self*, and her motives and thoughts led her into her actions. It would have been easy for her to get discouraged. The unsympathetic reactions of the people reminded her that she was an outcast and should not be in public. She might have wanted to leave, but she kept telling herself over and over again, "If I can just touch Him, I will be cured."

Truthful self talk has maintenance value to us. In other words, as we have truthful self talk, based on God's Word, it builds in us a maintenance value, so that when we find ourselves in difficulty, we can go back and remember what God has done. Like the woman who touched Jesus's robe, we can continue to speak encouragement to ourselves: "If I keep going to church, if I keep doing what's right, if I keep standing on the promise, if I hold true to what God says . . .I'm going to get through this." That's what the psalmist did in Psalm 42. He kept reminding himself, "I remember when I went to the temple. I remember how much joy I had. I remember how I led the singing." Our hope is in God. That has maintenance value to us.

Begin by trusting God in the small areas of life. Sometimes, that might be as simple as repeating, "God, I'm going to trust You today" instead of taking a Tylenol. Start trusting Him in small areas so that when the day comes for you to fight the giant, and the Goliath of sickness, divorce, or financial ruin is standing before you, you can remember. Like David, you can remember fighting a bear and a lion. You can remember that God delivered you. Your God is able to deliver you!

Make your inner voice a force of truthful, accurate, and positive thoughts for any false messages you have heard. You will hear those false messages continually everywhere in the world around you. So how can you make that inner voice speak truthful, accurate, positive thoughts for battling the false messages? There are four R's I use in my life to battle false messages: recognize, renounce, remove, and replace.

First, you have to **recognize** any misbelief. For example, locate any false messages regarding your worth. When was the first time you were told you were stupid? That destructive message spoken in jest or seriousness may have become embedded in your mind. As a child, I heard many negative remarks: "He doesn't do very well in school. He's not the sharpest pencil." As a result, I hated school. I was expelled in the first grade. My parents would take me to school, drop me off, and I'd beat them back home. I eventually quit school and went to work with my hands because they said, "Phil can fix anything. He's good with his hands. He talks a lot, but he's good with his hands."

> Know the difference between talking to yourself and letting yourself talk to you, and be aware of which one you're doing.

At the age of thirty I said, "I can do this school stuff. I am smart. I can read the Bible. I can understand it. I can write a paper and do research. I can do that." These are the things I began to tell myself. In the meantime, I married a woman who said, "You're the smartest of all the boys." And I started hearing my outward voice saying, "You can, you can, you can, you can."

Next, you have to **renounce** false beliefs. "Our marriage is not going to last. Everybody in our family gets divorced after five or six years. It's just the way we are." Renounce that false belief in the name of Jesus.

Then it's not good enough to just renounce those false beliefs in your mind. You have to **remove** them. Pull them down. And finallly, you must **replace** those false beliefs with positive thoughts. You don't get rid of a thought by saying, "I'm not going to feed that thought." You get rid of the thought by putting in another thought.

Some of you are sitting in bondage because you've allowed yourself and others to speak to you negatively: "God doesn't care. God doesn't have time for me. Maybe I'm going to go to heaven when I die, but who knows? This is just life's lot, and I've got to deal with it." No, Jesus said, "I want to give you abundant life." Whatever you tell your brain consistently, it will believe.

So how do we change the conversations? We change by repeating the truth whether we feel like it or not. Repeat the truth to yourself: "I am righteous, justified, loved, and worthy." That is biblical truth if you are a follower of Jesus. As we think on these things, the negative programming is taken captive. We cast out every thought that exalts itself against God, and every moment of every day we decide to make our inner voices forces of truthful, accurate, and positive thoughts for any and all false messages that might try and come against us.

The pages of Scripture are filled with stories of real flesh-and-blood people like you and me who often used self talk in their lives. For instance, in Psalm 57:8 the psalmist said, "Awake my soul." Then in Psalm 131:2, "I have stilled and quieted my soul." Psalm 103:2 says, "Oh, my soul, forget not all of His benefits." And in Psalm 116:7, "Be at rest once more, oh, my soul." Psalm 103:1, "Praise the Lord, oh, my soul." Judges 5:21, "March on, O my soul; be strong."

Unlike the psalmists, we often fail to say, "Awake, my soul," or "Put your hope and trust in God, my soul," or "Bless the Lord, O my soul." Instead, we say things like, "Well, it's going to be another one of those days," or "Nothing ever goes right for me," or "It's just my luck," usually inferring something negative. You rarely hear someone say, "Well, it's going to be another one of those wonderful days!" When someone says, "Today just isn't my day," I want to ask him or her, "Well, what do you mean when you say today isn't your day? You're breathing, right? You're living. Hey, if today wasn't your day, you'd be dead!"

To recap, I want to remind you of three powerful statements:

1. The most powerful voice in the universe to anyone is his or her own self talk. Earlier in this book, we talked about the difference between talking to yourself and letting yourself talk to you. It's often more powerful than God's voice because many times, even after God has told us something, it's our self talk that will talk us out of believing what God has told us.

Paul says in 2 Corinthians 5 and 10, "We demolish arguments, and every pretense that sets us up against the knowledge of God, and we take captive every thought to make it obedient to Christ." This is my challenge for you in this book: demolish those self arguments. Demolish those things that are contrary to what God's Word says.

2. In time, we become what we most believe about ourselves. It's our self talk, those things that we rehearse, those programs that become ingrained early on in our lives, that shape our reality. By the time we are eighteen years old, we have heard "No, you cannot do that" approximately 148,000 times, so we often never even try. Again, that's the reason it's important to demolish those strongholds. Take those arguments and pretenses that exalt themselves above the knowledge of God, and bring them into captivity.

Deuteronomy 29:29 says, "The secret things belong to the Lord. But the revealed things belong to us and to our children forever." *The secret things belong to the Lord.* What are the secret things? The secret things are those circumstances that we can't explain sometimes, that are unexpected and unavoidable. Those life events that seem to be ineffable. Secret things. The things that belong to the Lord. Those things for which we do not have an answer. Any time you ask, "God, why did this happen?" and you don't get a biblical reason or answer, and you can't trace it back to sin, Satan, or self, you've got to trust God because the secret things belong to Him.

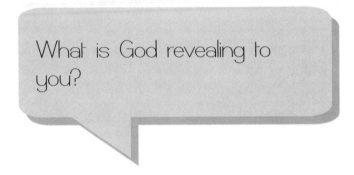

What is God revealing to you?

God said it is the *revealed* things that belong to us and to our children forever. Most of our lives are formed by the revealed things. Most of our lives are formed by those things that we read, hear, and that the Scripture tells us. Most of our lives are formed by those revealed things. You've likely heard the saying, "If it's meant to be, it's up to me." It's a cliché. A falsehood. I believe whatever *could* be is influenced by me. You see, everything that happens in our lives is not God's will. Whatever could be is going to be influenced by me.

In his book *Forces That Form Your Future*, Kevin Gerald wrote some questions to consider and ask ourselves. He said, "How different do you think your life would be today if your relationships had been different yesterday? If maybe your values had been different? Or maybe your words? How do you think your life would be altered had those things been different?" I believe your life would be radically changed.

Think about your decisions and your relationships and how they have brought you to this point in your life. Those same forces, relationships, beliefs, thoughts, and values that have shaped your life up to now will continue to shape your life tomorrow.

ACTION POINTS

1. How does meditating on the Word of God influence your self talk?

2. What steps can you take to make your inner voice a force of truth to counter all the false messages you hear on a daily basis?

3. How can using the four Rs improve your self talk?

CHAPTER 10

Getting Rid of the BS in Your Life

Whatever could be is influenced by me.

That's the reason that we must understand and examine our mind's programming. We view our present by the stories we tell ourselves about our past. The present is filtered through those things that we tell ourselves. Unfortunately, some of us have too much BS in our beliefs.

B.S. means Botched-up Self worth or Bad Self image. If you have botched-up self-worth or bad self-image, you have allowed the enemy, others, and even yourself to convince your mind that God does not have a plan for you, you were an accident, you don't have a future, and you can't make it in life. You must get rid of this wrong thinking, this BS, in your life. With God's help, past pains can be rewritten as battles won, not scars collected!

One of my parishioners sent me this email after I taught this series in my church:

> *Dear Pastor Phil,*
>
> *All of my life, I was told by my father in a crude and derogatory manner that I was ignorant. Every time I tried to speak, he would remind me that no one wanted to hear what I had to say because I was ignorant. I would try to share my dreams with my mother. My father would laugh out loud and tell me again how ignorant I was. For years, I have been an antisocial woman due to the beliefs he put in my head that carried over even into my own self talk. I would get excited and get ready to go for one of my dreams, and then I would talk myself out of it. There was just no way I could accomplish this because I'm not like everyone else. I would so badly want to encourage or to engage in adult conversations, but again, due to fear and self talk, I was ignored and nobody cared what I had to say. By experiencing death in my life, I began to move on with some of my dreams and a career and the courage to speak to other women. But after hearing this message, I am no longer waiting for another tragedy to move on.*

Sometimes, pain is a big motivator. God doesn't want you to be motivated by pain. He wants you to be motivated by *purpose*. He doesn't want you to hurt so much that you feel like you have to change. He wants you to get a revelation of what He says about you. He wants you to say, "You know what? I know God's got something big to do in my life."

Self talk is like an elevator. It can take you up, or it can take you down. Too many times we see ourselves struggling with botched self-worth because of those negative messages that we've heard and the negative things that we've lived through. Instead, we should wake up each day grateful that we have a pulse, and we can get out of bed. This is the day the Lord has made! We should say, "Thank You, God! I know You have something for me to do today." So what do we do about this? We need to bring our Big Five—our motives, attitudes, thoughts, words, and actions—into alignment with God and His Word.

> Your mind is a powerful force. Fill it with powerfully positive affirmations and truth!

Most of us know that we are where we are and we are what we are largely because of the dominating motives, attitudes, thoughts, words, and actions that have influenced us and that occupy our lives. We understand that if the majority of our lives are filled with negative motives, attitudes, thoughts, words, and actions, we have defeated our chances of succeeding in any area of life. We are not going anywhere in relationships, in our careers, or in our physical, emotional, or spiritual wellbeing. We must bring our minds into alignment with God's Word.

Anytime you are talking to someone, you can determine his or her future by simply asking two things. First, "Can he?"—a question that relates to his ability. And second, "Will he?"—a question that has to do with his attitude. Attitude always determines altitude.

When you are in Christ and have surrendered your life to Him, when you have said "yes" to the Lordship of Jesus Christ, then there is no question about your ability. There is no question about, "Can you?" Philippians 4:13 says you can do *all* things in Christ who gives you strength. God says, "I've declared you righteous before Me... I have blessed you with every spiritual blessing." So it's not a matter of ability. It always comes back to our attitude. Will we bring those motives, attitudes, thoughts, words, and actions into alignment with God's Word? Know this with assurance: your attitude is often determined by your self talk.

Many people struggle with the attitude of worthlessness. The attitude of worthlessness says, "I stink. I'm stupid. I'm ignorant." There are others who struggle with the attitude of lovelessness. That attitude of lovelessness says, "You stink. You're the problem. You're unloveable." Still others struggle with the attitude of bitterness. The attitude of bitterness says, "Life stinks. Nothing good will ever happen. Life is so unfair." You determine these attitudes.

If you have a poor sense of self-esteem or an attitude of worthlessness about yourself that repeats in your mind continually, "I stink. I'm a mistake. I never get any breaks. God doesn't love me," that attitude is going to take you right to the bottom of your life. You can be right with God in your heart, but you can be wrong with Him in your head. Understanding in your *heart* that you are right with God, that you are going to heaven when you die because you've confessed your sins and that you've accepted Jesus Christ, may not be enough if you don't get it right in your *head*. You will not enjoy life's journey or the freedom promised you through Christ. You're going to be saying, "Oh, God, I'll be glad when this world's done. I'll be glad when I die."

> Pay attention to your conversations.

Our minds are always thinking. The gears are clicking away in our heads. The gears in our minds should not out-turn God. Too often when our attitude in life is negative, the gears are turning and grinding the wrong way. When the gears in our minds are turning the wrong way, it leads to "stinkin' thinkin'." What we have to say is, "God, I want You to work in me. I don't want my gears to out-turn You in my head."

Worthlessness—"I stink." Lovelessness — "You stink." Bitterness —"Life stinks."

But God wants to help us get rid of our "stinkin' thinkin'" and BS Paul reminds us about our thoughts in Philippians 4. He says, "Finally, brothers, and whatever is true, and whatever is honorable, whatever is just, whatever is pure, whatever is lovely, whatever is gracious. If there is any excellence, if there is anything worthy of praise, think on these things." We

ACTION POINTS

1. Where can you identify the BS (botched self-worth) in your life that has kept you from being all you are called to be?

2. What conversations do you need to monitor more closely?

3. In what areas of your life do you see the "I stink, you stink, life stinks" attitude doing damage?

CHAPTER 11

Where Are You Now?

Now is the time to evaluate and take action on your self talk. There are six things to keep in mind as you begin to change your thought patterns. Here they are:

1. Change always starts in the mind. Our behavior changes when our thinking changes. The way we think is always going to determine the way we feel. The way we feel is going to be determined by the way we act, but it all begins with our thoughts. When our thinking gets right, our feelings get right. If you can change your thoughts, you will change your life. Change starts in the mind.

2. To change our minds, we must change our beliefs. We have to attack the BS (botched self-worth) in our beliefs. We must rid ourselves of the botched self-image that has driven some of us since we were children. We must confront our thoughts and speak truth from God's Word: "Wait a minute. This is not the way God designed things. God didn't design me to live and think like this."

In John 8:32 Jesus said, "You will know the truth and it will set you free." God's truth, as recorded in the Bible, will set us free when we align ourselves with it. This book is not about positive thinking or about trying to be the little engine that could: "I think I can, I think I can, I think I can." Instead, this book is about aligning ourselves with the Word of God by saying, "God, I want to make Your Word the priority in my life." I challenge you to read through the Bible this year and discover the truths God has for your life. You are not going to remember everything you read. But as you read through the Bible, highlight some verses that you can return to later and study. The Bible will lead you to God's way of thinking, His beliefs, and then you will be able to find His perspective on your life. When you know God's perspective, you can begin to change your beliefs.

3. Behind every sin, there is a lie that we believe. In Genesis 3:10 Adam talks to God. He says, "I heard Your voice in the garden. And I was afraid because I was naked, so I hid myself." And God said, "Who told you that you were naked?" God approached Adam and said, "Wait a minute. Who told you? Where did you get this information?" Behind every sin is a lie that people believe. We have to be willing to attack the lie behind the behavior. Satan lied in Genesis 3. It was a two-fold lie. First, he said, "God lies to His children." And second, Satan told Eve, "There aren't any consequences to your behavior anyway." We know better. We know that eternity means just that. Forever. That's a long time to pay for believing a lie! Don't believe the lies Satan whispers to you.

Do you see how we have to be careful? Whatever happens to me is influenced by me. I have to be willing to say, "Wait a minute. I need to attack this lie." Who told you that you are stupid? Who told you that you are incapable? God wants us to know, "It wasn't Me because you are made in My likeness. You're made in My image. I created you. I sanctioned you. I formed you. I've given you a purpose and a destiny."

Paul said in Titus 3:3, "At one time, we too were foolish, disobedient, deceived, and enslaved by all kinds of passions and pleasures." But then... "the kindness, and the favor, and the love of God, our Savior appeared." We can be deceived by self talk. We can allow people to put negative things in our minds. We can believe the lie of our culture and the lie of our society that we can do as we please, as long as we're not hurting anyone.

When Christ appears in your life, do you know what He does? He attacks the deception. He attacks it. If someone has been unfaithful or uncommitted, one might wonder what lie is behind their behavior. What untruths have they been told?

4. Trying to change someone's behavior without changing his beliefs is a waste of time. If you ask a person to change before his mind is renewed, change will never occur. A guy went into a tattoo parlor, and observed one tattoo that said, "Born to lose." He asked the tattoo artist, "Is there anybody who would really put 'Born to lose' on their skin?" The tattoo artist replied, "Hey, before I tattoo it on their skin, it is already tattooed on their minds."

Trying to change our behavior without changing our beliefs is futile. Why? Because our beliefs have a BS (botched self-worth) factor. They are filled with this botched-up stuff that we've heard from others and ourselves. What happens is this. Every time we hear something, every time we say something, electrical pulses are created in our brains. They begin to create a rut. The more you hear something, the more you think something, and the easier it is to think that error. A rut has been formed. Every time you have untrue thoughts, it creates a deeper rut. If you want to see change, you must get out of those ruts and change your auto-pilot! You may acknowledge that you shouldn't think a certain way, and you may try to change by sheer will power, but an untruth, repeated continually by yourself or others, becomes programmed into your brains.

For example, a wife may convince her husband that he needs to change and attend church more frequently. It may work for a while as he attends church with her and uses his will power to say, "I'm not going to curse. I'm not going to carouse. I'm not going to drink." But if his belief system doesn't change, if he hasn't attacked the lie that is behind his behavior and hasn't dealt with his BS, or botched self-worth, then the moment he lets down his guard, his mind will go back to automatic pilot.

The biblical term for change is "repentance." The Greek word for change is *metanoia*, which means to change your mind. Repentance isn't just changing the way *we* think about something. It's changing the way *God* thinks about it. To repent means to say, "God, You are going to be the final authority. You are going to be the final word in my life. You are going to be the Alpha and the Omega to me. I'm going to repent. I'm going to change the way that I think."

Repentance is a paradigm shift. God is in the paradigm shift business. He's in the "changing" business. He longs for people to repent. Repentance means coming to God and saying, "The way I've been thinking about You, Lord, the way I've been thinking about myself and others, the way that I've been thinking about life, isn't right. I'm going to change. I'm going to repent. I'm going to think the way You want me to think about everything."

5. We don't change people's minds. The applied Word of God does. We can't argue people into change. We can't sit people down and attempt to theologically convince them with our arguments. It's the applied Word of God that will make the difference. When you know the truth, it's the truth you know and apply to your life that will change you. If I could change minds about self-worth and self talk and influence wasn't necessary, I wouldn't wait for you to read this book. I'd post it on Facebook. I'd zap you! Be changed in the name of Jesus! Some people go to church every Sunday, They know the truth, they believe the truth, and they receive the truth. Life change begins to happen for them. There are other people who do the same, but they don't believe the truths they hear. They can't wipe out the past conversations that ring in their heads. The Word of God has not been applied in their lives, and it is this applied Word that changes people.

> Let God dictate your conversations. We don't change people's minds. The Word of God does.

6. Changing our motives, attitudes, thoughts, words, and actions is the fruit of repentance. Repentance isn't a change of behavior, but behavior change is a result of repentance. We don't change our behavior when we say, "Oh, God, I repent of the negative ways I've been thinking. I repent of my deeds." No, behavior change is a result of that repentance.

Matthew 3:8 says, "Produce fruit in keeping with repentance." The result of that changed heart is that my motives, my attitudes, my thoughts, my words, and my actions, can *now* be put in alignment with God's Word. I have lined them up with God's Word. I begin to process my thoughts as God wants them to be processed in my life. Then the fruit of repentance begins to produce.

God wants thoughts to be processed in our minds in order to lead to the fruit of repentance. The concept of garbage in and garbage out isn't something that just happens to computers. Our minds are the greatest computers in the world. We have programmed many things into our minds, and if we don't reprogram them, we will produce the garbage that has been programmed in. When I have a problem in my spiritual life, I can inevitably trace it to an undisciplined mind. When garbage comes out, it's because garbage has gone in.

Biblically correct thinking challenges the "I stink, you stink, life stinks" worldview. There are three steps to biblically correct thinking. The first choice that must be made to ensure biblically correct thinking involves changing the worthlessness mentality. To change that mentality we must think about the good, true, and right that Paul reminded us about in Philippians. Your truth must come from God's Word, not from your feelings because feelings are deceptive.

My feelings often take control of me. I can preach a message on Sunday and feel good about it. My congregants shake my hand after the service and say, "Pastor, you really blessed me. You spoke to my heart and ministered to me." But by Tuesday, one negative email that says, "You were too long, It was too loud. You move too much (or you don't move enough)," can cause me to lose all good feelings and leave me with an "I stink" attitude.

Christ is not the accuser of the brethren. Satan is the accuser. Christ is about acceptance. He doesn't approve of your sin. He wants you to acknowledge your sin and come to Him for forgiveness, but His arms are wide open. He's full of acceptance. As the accuser, Satan is the one who gets in your self talk and uses it to condemn you: "God's not going to hear you. God's not going to bless you." Align your thoughts with God's Word. He accepts you. God will lift you up. He will heal you.

Psalm 139 says, "I praise You for I am fearfully and wonderfully made. Marvelous are Your works. And that, my soul knows well." Is it really surprising to our culture that when God was taken out of the public school setting, our kids could be told that they are animals, and they act like animals? The Bible says children are fearfully and wonderfully made. Is it really surprising to our culture that when we took prayer and the Bible out of school that test scores started hitting bottom? Leaving God out of life's equation negates His assurance that we are made in His image. Our souls need to be reminded from God's Word that we are fearfully and wonderfully made. Attack the negative thinking head-on, and remind yourself that you do not stink!

Christ died so we could experience God's acceptance, not His accusation. A theology of doubt, despair, hopelessness, and fear is not from God. Some have forgotten the good news of the gospel! Think thoughts that are right, or actually *righteous*. Stop the gears from turning the wrong way. Ephesians 2:10 says, "For we are God's own handiwork, His workmanship as recreated in Christ Jesus, born anew that we may do those good works which God predestined for us, taking paths which He prepared ahead of time, that we should walk in them, living the good life which He prearranged and made ready for us to live." Here is a list of truths from God's Word that will change your thinking. Dwell on them. Make them a part of your thinking and your life. Align your mind with God's by believing these truths:

1. You are made in the image of God and after His likeness.

2. God knew you before you were formed in your mother's womb.

3. You are a chosen instrument of God.

4. You are to continually praise God.

5. You are fearfully and wonderfully made.

6. You can do marvelous things through Him.

7. God planned in advance for you to do good works.

8. You were created to enjoy the good life that God has prepared.

9. You are somebody because "God don't make junk."

Start the gears turning the right way. Choose to think biblically right about yourself.

Second, biblically correct thinking about my family and my friends is important. Most of us know, it's so easy to be harsh and critical about people whom we are supposed to love. It's so easy to accentuate the negative in the lives of others. It's so easy to find ourselves pointing out the flaws and faults in our children. Rather than fixating on their faults and communicating these feelings, we take God's perspective. These are people for whom He died, whom He loves to eternity. People who are God's children. These little ones will be men and women of God someday. God is going to raise them up and do mighty things in their lives. I appeal to you as a parent or a grandparent, do not be cursing your babies. Don't put unkind thoughts and words in their minds. All kids mess up, but to fixate and communicate always on their flaws will cause eternal harm. And if you are one of those adults who is still fixated on the unkind remarks of your childhood, remember that the past is over. By the grace of God, you are moving forward. You are in the healing process.

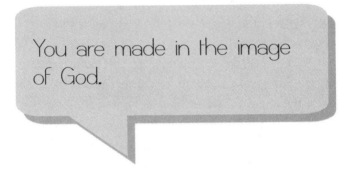

You are made in the image of God.

Biblically correct thinking about other people involves not judging them. Paul said it like this in 1 Corinthians 4:5: "Therefore, don't go passing judgment before the time. But wait until the Lord comes. He will bring to light those things in the darkness and expose the motives of men's hearts. And then each man's praise shall come to him from God." It is God who will expose the motives of people's hearts.

Mom and Dad, you only have your babies with you for a while. What you are experiencing now, what they're hearing from you now, the words that you're putting on them now, are going to affect them for their entire lives. You realize this as an adult because you've been there. Unfortunately, some of us are now passing on the same negative and destructive words that were said to us. Stop it. Ask God to help you. Bring your motives, thoughts, attitudes, words, and actions into alignment with God's Word so that the things you think about your family are lovely and pure. Even when you want to choke them to death, choke them with love.

Third, biblically correct thinking about our circumstances is necessary. An attitude of bitterness as a result of our circumstances will destroy us. Think thoughts that are lovely, pure, and honorable. We can learn a powerful lesson from the life of a girl named Bubbles.

Her friends called her Bubbles, but she had every reason to be bitter. She was a talented yet unrecognized opera singer. Many of the opera companies in the United States ignored her compelling voice. She was rejected for parts for which she was easily qualified. It was not until Bubbles went to Europe that she won the hearts of the toughest to please—the European audiences.

Stateside opinion leaders began to acknowledge her talent, but Bubbles not only had a professional battle, she had a personal battle. She was professionally rejected, and she had many personal setbacks and problems. Bubbles was the mother of two handicapped children. One was severely mentally disabled. In order to escape the hectic pace of life in New York, she purchased a home in Martha's Vineyard. It burned to the ground two days before she was going to move there. Every one of these things was perfect soil for sowing the seeds of bitterness and negativity. But her friends didn't call her Bitter. They called her Bubbles. Her real name was Beverly Sills. She died in 2007 at the age of 78.

Before her death, reporters interviewed her about all the setbacks and struggles in her life. When asked how she handled those problems, Beverly said, "I choose to be cheerful." She said, "Years ago, I knew I had little or no choice about my success and my circumstances. I knew I could not choose what happens *to* me, but I could choose what happens *in* me. I choose things to think about that are noble, that are relevant, that are lofty, that are not mundane, that are not common. I choose to meditate on those things. That's how I live my life."

It radically changes us when we say, "God, let me attack that worthlessness attitude. With the Word of God, I don't stink. I want to think things that are true and right. I am made in the image of God." Attack those "you stink" attitudes of lovelessness. Instead say, "God, I want to think things that are lovely. Let me attack the bitterness that goes on in my life. God, I want to always think about things that are honorable."

I love Jeremiah 32:40-41: "I'll make an everlasting covenant with them. I will not turn away from them to do them good. I will rejoice over them to do them good." This is God's view of you. We must train ourselves to think thoughts about our circumstances that are biblically correct. Are you convinced that God is good even when it seems that life stinks?

Did you ever play with Play-Doh? Do you know its history?

In 1930, a guy by the name of Noah McVicker invented Play-Doh originally as wallpaper cleaner. It came only in white. He made very little money with it. He almost went bankrupt because he couldn't succeed with wallpaper cleaner. He had a nephew, named Joe, who returned from the war. Joe showed up at his uncle's place of business, saw this Play-Doh, and took some home. Joe discovered that his children would rather play with the Play-Doh than with their old, hard, dry clay.

Noah and Joe made one adjustment and introduced their product as Play-Doh. By the age of 27, Joe McVicker became a millionaire after releasing this product as a toy rather than wallpaper cleaner. The rest is history. Play-Doh has been in almost every home in America. Making one adjustment radically changed their future.

Some of you are just one adjustment away from radically changing your lives. You may be just one adjustment away from radically changing your life this year. Your success is dependent upon the realization that God says there is something powerful in you. Make that your self talk. Bringing your motives, thoughts, attitudes, words, and actions into alignment with God's Word will be the one adjustment that can radically change your life.

Jesus said in John 16:33, "In Me, you may have peace. In the world, you're going to have tribulations. But take care of your reach. I have overcome the world." The peace of God does not come from transcendental meditation or yoga. It doesn't come from religion or human relationship or financial security. Peace can only be found in relationship with Jesus Christ. God never gives us anything that makes Him unnecessary! Some people will seek what they desire in another person, but Jesus said, "In Me, you're going to have peace."

True peace can only be found in Jesus Christ. He is called the Prince of Peace! When there is no Christ, you have no peace. But when you know Christ, you know peace. I don't care where you go, what you do, what the numbers are on your salary, or what subdivision you live in. There is not a big enough house that can readily give you the peace that you want in your life. That peace only comes from Christ. No Christ, no peace. Know Christ and know peace. Make one adjustment. Get rid of the BS in your life. Get rid of that botched self-worth. Stop saying, "I stink, you stink, life stinks." God reminds us, "I have overcome this world."

ACTION POINTS

1. What lie can you identify behind any destructive behavior that keeps you from living a life of victory and success?

2. Can you identify with the frustration of trying to change a person's behavior without having their belief system changed?

3. What is the one thing you can do today to begin the process of change in a difficult circumstance or relationship?

CHAPTER 12

Impact

THE TOPIC OF this book has been the impact that our own words and thoughts, as well as the words of others, have on our lives. This is not a book about positive thinking because it is not only about trying to make positive affirmations in your lives. We've been talking about how we make biblical confessions. How do we confess with our mouths the truth of God's Word? When we begin to confess out loud the promises of God, we start releasing the blessing of God over our hearts and lives. That has a powerful impact.

We have learned the importance of guarding our mouths. Remember, Proverbs 18:20 says that life and death are in the tongue. The tongue has the power of life, or it has the power of death. The most powerful voice in this universe to any one person is their own self talk. Many times God speaks to us, but we don't listen. We have trained ourselves with our self talk, those things we say to ourselves or perhaps the things that someone else has said to us.

Paul Meyer said this: "You are what you think about all day long." What we think about, we bring about. This gives a new dimension to understanding Proverbs 13:3, which says, "He who guards his mouth preserves his life. But he who speaks rashly will come to ruin." It is not always the wisest thing to say what you think. "Honey, does this dress make my behind look big?" The only possible answer to that question is "No," in case you wondered. He who guards his mouth preserves his life. This proverb implicates the destructive self talk we can level at ourselves and others on a daily basis. Every word in our lives is like a seed. We won't grow what we don't sow! Guarding our hearts or guarding our spirit is equivalent to guarding the things that we sow into them. I have often been preserved by saying nothing, but he who speaks rashly will come to ruin.

Guarding our heart or guarding our spirit is equivalent to simply guarding the things upon which we feed. Everything in your life is a seed. We don't grow what we don't sow. When you have negative things sown into your life, you're going to grow negative results. When you have positive things sown into your life, you're going to have positive results.

Make an impact on the world with your words.

Look at Proverbs 15:4: "A wholesome tongue is the tree of life, but perverseness in the tongue breaks the spirit." Have you ever witnessed a parent breaking the spirit of a child with his or her words? Sure you have. We have also seen grown women and men have their spirits broken by words. Proverbs 16:24 confirms, "Pleasant words are like honeycomb, sweetness to the soul and health to the bones." Proverbs 12:18 says, "There is one who speaks like the piercing of a sword but the tongue of the wise promotes hell." Again, the Scriptures make it clear that our spiritual lives, our physical lives, our emotional lives, and our relational lives stem from the proper use of our tongue, whether the tongue is used for self talk, for what we say to somebody else, or for what we allow to be said to us. The Scriptures are filled with examples of people who used words both to encourage and discourage themselves and other people. If hidden in your heart, the Word of God will sustain you.

One example in Scripture of the tongue's use as an instrument of encouragement is found in Job 4. We learn that Job had a healing quality about his words. Eliphaz, one of Job's friends, says, "Think of how you have instructed many, how you have strengthened feeble hands, your words have upheld him who was stumbling and you have strengthened the feeble man." How did Job do that? With his words.

Look at another example, Isaiah. He used his power of speech to give strength to the weary. Isaiah said about himself in Isaiah 15:4, "The Lord has given me the tongue of the learned. Then I should know how to speak in the season to him who was weary." In other words, Isaiah said that because God gave him the ability to discern, he was able to speak to people in a weary season. He knew what to say. When our children make mistakes, the last thing they need to hear from us is "You messed up." The first thing they need to hear is "I love you." We have to have discernment to be able to do that.

So words can encourage us, but words can also intimidate. They can start an epidemic of panic and discouragement. Again, the Bible gives us many examples of the power of the tongue. God noticed His people in Deuteronomy 1:27 who murmured in their tents.

Our words can encourage or they can discourage. Yet we are called upon to repair and fortify the spiritual walls of our minds against the negative self talk generated by ourselves or other people. That's the reason Paul tells us in 2 Corinthians 10:5, "We demolish arguments and every pretense that sets itself up against the knowledge of God and we take captive every thought to make it obedient to Christ."

Don't tell me you're struggling if you're not fighting! Some people don't struggle. They just surrender, saying, "Well, this is the way I am. This is the way I talk. This is the way I was raised." They just surrender to what they think is inevitable. Paul said we have to fight against these things. It's not going to be automatic for us. When we hear negative and destructive things, we must filter them. The best way to filter the negativity is to bring our motives, attitudes, thoughts, words, and actions into alignment with God's Word. Remember, we get rid of the BS, that botched self-worth. We get rid of that bad self talk. Remember to ask yourself, "What does God's Word say about negative self talk? How can I train myself so that my words can be an encouragement to me and to others?"

We all want to be encouraged. Most of us don't get up in the morning and say, "Okay, God, I want to have every negative thought that I possibly can about my life today." No, you don't do that! You want to get up every day and say, "God, I want to receive what You want me to have today! I want to be able to inherit what You have positioned for me today! I want to fulfill the purpose today that You've given me." How do I do that? I bring my Big Five motives, attitudes, thoughts, words, and actions, into alignment with God's Word.

ACTION POINTS

1. What are two positive affirmations you can make to yourself that will help change the impact you can have on others?

2. Who do you have right now in your sphere of influence that would benefit from words of encouragement?

3. In what area of your Big Five life have you been surrendering instead of fighting?

CHAPTER 13

Action

So how do we get rid of twisted thinking? Some refer to this as cognitive distortion. I like to call it twisted thinking. Distorted thinking can come from the words or actions of others or from our own self talk. Your identity is in God, not in the DNA of man. But it is human nature to compare ourselves and our identities to the family members who raised us or came before us.

This is not God's view of you. God created you as a unique individual with your own traits, inherent DNA, and calling on your life. Only you can stand in the way of that inheritance by offering excuses for why you think negatively or allow inaction or twisted thinking to interrupt your calling. The focus of Proverbs 4:23 is guarding your heart, taking action, and keeping your greatest assets healthy. Is your thinking healthy and guided in the direction God wants you to go?

As a pastor I've heard many different examples of thinking that just isn't healthy. One man said, "When I was a child, my dad abused me and my mom every day. Can I become a loving husband and father?" Here's another one: "My dad wasn't around growing up. He took off when I was little. Do I have what it takes to stick it out in my relationship?" Another said, "My dad was never at home. He spent all of his time working. Can I be successful and still have a happy, fulfilled family life?"

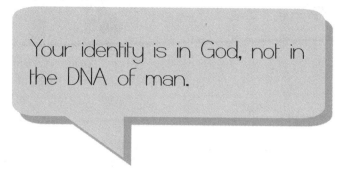

Your identity is in God, not in the DNA of man.

Again, what we see modeled sometimes is what we end up passing on. Here's one: "I had a great dad growing up but now that I'm older, I see some character flaws in him that I don't want to repeat. Can I avoid these areas?" And, "My dad died when I was little. I really miss not having a dad. Can I still grow up into a man without having a father figure in my life?" Or, "My dad hated God. Can I really have an intimate, personal relationship with God?"

In every one of these remarks, I see a pattern that simply says, "I don't want to repeat this destructive path." Maybe you are a born-again believer. Maybe you've moved on from some of the baggage you have carried in your mind. Maybe you've been able to have some healing and help from God. But if you are not careful, you will keep passing that same garbage to your children. Allow God to take your attitudes, motives, thoughts, words, and actions and bring them under submission and alignment with the Word of God every day. Otherwise, you will find yourself repeating with your children what happened to you. Twisted thinking can cause us to struggle with this.

The Bible has identified at least eight twisted types of thinking that can entrap us, distort our view of life, and keep us from becoming what God wants us to be. In order to get rid of the BS (botched self-worth) and the bad, barren, broken self-image, we must be willing to confront some of this twisted thinking right up front and say, "Lord, help me to bring my thoughts and my mind into alignment with Your Word. Help me to remember Your truths so that I do not believe and live with lies. Help me to plan my life each day to bring honor to You."

The first twisted thinking distortion is called "all-or-nothing thinking." This occurs when we always see things in black and white. All-or-nothing thinking describes a person who comes to church and wants to follow Christ, but he or she says, "If I can't be perfect all the time, then it must mean that I'm a failure. If I can hit on all cylinders, it must mean I didn't get anything." Some people pass this all-or-nothing thinking on to other people.

Cain struggled with this. In Genesis 4:3–7, the Bible says,

> Through the process of time, it came to pass, that Cain brought an offering of the fruit of the ground to the Lord,

and Abel, also brought the firstborn of his flock and of their fat and the Lord respected Abel in his offering but he did not respect Cain's offering, and Cain was very angry and his countenance fell. So the Lord said to Cain, Why are you angry? Why had your countenance fallen? If you do well, will you not be accepted? If you do not do well, sin lies at the door, and its desire is for you but you should rule over it, Cain.

But Cain had this all-or-nothing view. Cain knew the process of sacrifice. I am convinced that he knew, as Abel knew, what God required. He required the best. He required the first fruits. This is more than just Cain saying, "Dad and Mom love Abel more than they love me." Hebrews 11 says that by *faith* Abel offered his sacrifice to God. It was by faith. The Bible says what is not of faith is sin, right? The Bible says we walk by faith, not by sight. Here is Cain, knowing what God requires, *knowing*, and God called his hand. God said, "Cain, why are you angry? Why has your countenance fallen? You know that if you do well you are going to be accepted." But Cain had this all-or-nothing mindset.

Three things need to happen when you have this all-or-nothing thinking. First, take responsibility. Acknowledge it's your fault. Second, repent. Ask God for forgiveness. And third, trust God to take a mistake and turn it into a miracle or a blessing.

Take action to eliminate twisted thinking, not only in your own life but in the lives of others through your leadership and mentoring.

Matthew 25:18, 24–27 gives the story of the talents. It's the same scenario there. This all-or-nothing guy had five talents, and he multiplied that amount by five more. Another fellow had two talents, and he doubled it. The last man said, "I'm fearful," so he prayed and hid the money in the ground. Their master came to evaluate what they had done with his money. The first two were commended, but the last man was held accountable for his laziness. He should have trusted God and trusted his master. This fearful servant could only think in terms of success or failure, rich or poor. It's like saying, "If I cannot be Bill Gates or Donald Trump, then I am a failure."

Success is not a matter of having great largess or stakes of wealth. We do not have to be Rockefellers, Duponts, Ross Perot, or Bill Gates. We can be landscape workers or guard rail contractors, or even obscure English teachers in deep East Texas. These either/or distortions come in the form of dichotomies such as liberal/conservative, Protestant/Catholic, fundamentalist/orthodox. Peter fell into it in John 13:5–9.

After that, He poured water into a basin and began to wash the disciples' feet, and to wipe them with the towel with which He was girded. Then He came to Simon Peter. And Peter said to Him, "Lord, are You washing my feet?" Jesus answered and said to him, "What I am doing you do not understand now, but you will know after this." Peter said to Him, "You shall never wash my feet!" Jesus answered him, "If I do not wash you, you have no part with Me." Simon Peter said to Him, "Lord, not my feet only, but also my hands and my head!"

We see this twisted thinking at work. It wasn't about Jesus giving Peter a bath. Jesus wanted Peter to learn that it's not all-or-nothing always.

If you are not a total success, it doesn't mean that you are a failure. You do not have to condemn yourself if you do not keep every aspect of what is required. "Well, I tried reading the Bible, pastor. You know, I got a few days behind, and I just quit." Why? All-or-nothing thinking. Sometimes people tell me, "Well, I won't come to Jesus until I know I can give Him 100 percent." Start with fifty! Start with something.

People do it all the time with tithing. "Oh, I can't give 10 percent. There's just no way." They feel guilty, and they don't even try. Start somewhere. This all-or-nothing thinking is deadly and destructive. Take responsibility and do something.

We see this all-or-nothing thinking in the Corinthian congregation when the matter of degree could not be seen in the punishment/forgiveness dichotomy (2 Corinthians 2:6–8). Ironically, these people thought they were loving the man by tolerating his sin. When the man had genuinely repented, the Corinthian congregation went to the opposite extreme of hard-nosed intolerance. This kind of all-or-nothing thinking causes us to fixate on our sins, rather than having a more balanced view of our spiritual life and God's grace.

Another great story that illustrates this all-or-nothing idea can be found in Genesis 16. Sarah was unable to have a baby through Abraham, even though God promised she would. Sarah got restless. She came to Abraham and said, "Abraham, I have this servant Hagar. I want to give Hagar to you. Go lay with her, and we'll have a child through her." You know the story. Hagar has a baby. Ishmael is born, and there's tension in the house. Imagine that!

Sarah blames Abraham, mistreats Hagar and Ishmael, and over the next several years complains about something that would have never happened had she not suggested it. Ishmael became an undeniable part of their lives, for the rest of their lives. How would that scenario have changed had Sarah gone to God, taken responsibility, repented, and sought forgiveness? How different the end of the story might have been if Sarah had confessed her mistake to God and acknowledged that He could turn it into a blessing.

The world's culture would be radically different today if Sarah had not planted that seed of animosity between Isaac and Ishmael. The descendants of those two boys are still fighting each other. All-or-nothing thinking is destructive. It is impossible to hit it 100 percent correct every day, seven days a week, 365 days a year. Take responsibility when you sin, and cry to God for forgiveness: "God, take this mistake and turn it into a blessing!" What if we could move beyond "sin conscience to seed conscience"? We won't grow what we don't sow.

The second twisted-thinking distortion is overgeneralization. Overgeneralization occurs when someone sees a **single negative event and overgeneralizes it into a never-ending pattern of defeat.** Usually, when we come to a sweeping, negative conclusion that far surpasses the significance of the actual event, we have overgeneralized. One overgeneralization I've heard in churches is this: "Pastor, do you want to know why I don't go to church? Well, it's because everybody at church is a hypocrite." *Really, everybody?* I respond, "Now on what basis have you made this decision?" I might get an answer like this: "Forty years ago, I went to church when I was ten years old, and there was this guy, a man who was a deacon. He would curse and do some bad things." Over-generalization. Everybody's a jerk because you know *one*? Really?

The Israelites fell into this twisted thinking in the Sinai. At the first sign of frustration they overgeneralized about their situation. Exodus 16:3 says, "The Israelites said to them, 'If only we had died by the LORD's hand in Egypt! There we sat around pots of meat and ate all the food we wanted, but you have brought us out into this desert to starve this entire assembly to death.'" One negative event and the entire assembly saw it as a continuous pattern of defeat. God had just brought them out of Egypt and demonstrated miracle after miracle. No wonder God calls them children. God had proven Himself to them over and over. God still proves Himself to you.

In relationships overgeneralizing can be particularly destructive. Comments like "He never..." or "she never..." or "She always..." are greatly over-generalized. In a marriage relationship, the "he/she never..." can be a statement that destroys the marriage. An overgeneralized statement is another form of a negative thought. We must rethink our words and reconsider the circumstances.

There are always some gray areas if you look for them. You can say something like this: "I can love my wife and still get upset at her." It doesn't have to be an either/or statement like, "Oh, he got upset at me today. He doesn't love me." No, it doesn't mean he doesn't love you.

There are parts of my life that I enjoy, and there are parts of my life that create stress. My children bring me great joy, but they sometimes drive me crazy. Have you heard some parents say, "My kids just drive me crazy all the time!" Really? *All* the time? No, not all the time! They drive you crazy *sometimes*, and there are also good times, right? These over-generalizations are destructive in our lives. They keep us from moving where God wants us to move.

The third twisted thinking distortion involves the mental filter that we often use when we pick out a single negative detail and we dwell on it exclusively. When we do this, our vision of reality becomes darkened. It's like a drop of ink that discolors the entire pan of water. A great example of this can be found in Genesis 3. God had given Adam and Eve many things in the garden that they could eat, touch, climb, and enjoy. God told them that they were not to eat of *one* tree in this garden. But they decided to obsess about the *one* thing they could not have.

Genesis 3:1-3 says,

> Now the serpent was more cunning than any beast of the field which the LORD God had made. And he said to the tellswoman, "Has God indeed said, 'You shall not eat of every tree of the garden'?" And the woman said to the

serpent, "We may eat the fruit of the trees of the garden; but of the fruit of the tree which is in the midst of the garden, God has said, 'You shall not eat it, nor shall you touch it, lest you die.'"

Satan diverted Eve's attention to the one exception in the garden. Eve fixates in her mental filter on the one thing God told them *not* to eat instead of all the things that they could eat. Our mental filter is important to how we discern the details in our lives. Remember, it isn't what happens to you, it's the story that you tell yourself about what happens to you that is going to determine your success or your defeat. God said don't touch the fruit of that one tree. The story that Eve told herself was, "God said don't touch it. God says don't eat of it. God has made this totally impossible for us."

Another great story in the New Testament is found in Luke 15. It's the story of the prodigal son who was lost and returns home. A great feast is held on the return of the prodigal son to his home. The elder son is there, and he becomes upset, saying, "All these many years I've been serving you, Father, and I never transgressed your commandment, and you never gave me a young goat that I might make merry with my friends. As soon as the youngest son comes home, even though he has devoured his livelihood, you killed the fatted cow for him." The father replies, "Son, you've always been with me. You never wanted to have a party. You could have had a party every day!" The eldest son fixates on this one calf. His mental filter is focused on this one thing. He tries to project upon his dad what he perceives as a lack of love, "You don't love me like you love my baby brother."

Some people feel like God doesn't love them like he loves other people. Upon consideration you will admit that God's grace and mercy in your life have been abundant. We have to be careful that we don't pick out a single negative detail and dwell on it exclusively. This principle holds true for marriage, for raising children, and for all aspects of life and relationships.

A fourth pattern of twisted thinking is disqualifying the positive. Again, a positive experience is rejected by insisting that it doesn't count for some reason or other. An act of God's will may be discounted. With this twisted thinking we maintain a negative belief even when it is contradicted by our everyday experience.

Moses is a great example. In Exodus 4, when Moses is eighty years old, God tells him that He is going to use him to lead His people out of Egypt. Moses counters, "God, You know I'm not eloquent. You spoke of me as a servant but I'm slow of speech, and I'm slow of tongue. Oh, I'm so humble." Humility is a godly trait, but artificial humility or self-deprecation is not ever going to help us succeed. This wasn't the place for it. God knew about Moses. Yet Moses rejected something positive from God in his life. God had kept him for eighty years from the time he was a baby in the Nile River. Moses should have believed and followed God's instructions without question.

I began preaching when I was sixteen. I'd been involved with a singing ministry, but I never preached. I was very nervous before my first message. A minister came to me and said, "Phil, if God used Balaam's ass, I think He's got a chance with you."

There is perception, and then there is the reality. Just because we see and feel things in a certain way, it doesn't mean that it's always reality. Your perception can be wrong sometimes, and often it is when it comes to what God wants to do in your life. God hasn't written you off. God hasn't said there's no use for you. The reality is that God does great things if only people would submit themselves to Him. He takes nobodies and makes somebodies out of them.

Seeing a situation for what it really is, instead of what it feels like, can help us stay grounded. But magnifying a problem only gives it more energy and provides the opportunity for the situation to become larger than it was ever intended to be.

The fifth distortion of twisted thinking is the pattern of jumping to conclusions. Jumping to conclusions involves making negative interpretations of what someone says without having all the facts. There are two aspects of jumping to conclusions. One is **mind reading**.

Have you ever had the experience of thinking you know what someone else is thinking just by how they look at you? In other words, you claimed to read their minds: "Oh, I know what he was thinking. I know exactly what he's thinking." We jump to conclusions sometimes to our own destruction.

A great story about this problem is in 1 Samuel 1. The priest Eli was guilty of mind reading when he watched the behavior of Hannah. As he went into the temple, he saw Hannah, who was praying. Eli watched her mouth as she continued praying before the Lord. Hannah spoke in her heart to the Lord and only her lips moved. Her voice was not heard. Therefore, Eli thought she was drunk. Eli said to her, "How long will you be drunk? Put the wine away." She wasn't drunk. Hannah was crying out silently to the Lord. She longed to have a son, but she was unable to become pregnant. Eli made an incorrect assumption about her. Mind reading.

The second aspect of jumping to conclusions is fortune-telling. Fortune-telling involves anticipating that things will turn out badly. We feel that our prediction is an already established fact.

Deuteronomy 1:27 says, "And you complained in your tents, and said, 'Because the LORD hates us, He has brought us out of the land of Egypt to deliver us into the hand of the Amorites, to destroy us,'" It was the jumping to conclusions and mind reading of the Israelites that gave them this distorted and twisted view of God.

Have you ever had people jump to conclusions about things in your life? Have you ever jumped to conclusions about someone else's life? Don't judge people until you've walked in their shoes. Don't allow other people to judge you until they understand the facts. Sometimes you have a heart for God, and you pray, and you seek God, and you fast, and you read the Scriptures, and you do everything you possibly can, but life may not happen the way you want it to. Don't jump to conclusions and think that God is against you! Get all the facts.

A sixth distortion of twisted thinking involves magnifying and minimizing. We often exaggerate even our own goof ups. Don't magnify a situation. For instance, "Oh, I tell you, we had the worst fight ever. I just know our marriage is going downhill. We're going to get a divorce. That'll be the end." Magnifying the situation is never helpful. Also, sometimes we minimize our own or someone else's success. When we magnify our defeats or minimize our successes, the road has been paved to destruction because neither are accurate views of our lives or the lives of others.

A classic magnification distortion occurred with our forebears on Sinai. Numbers 13:31–33 records it this way:

> But the men who had gone up with him said, "We are not able to go up against the people, for they are stronger than we." And they gave the children of Israel a bad report of the land which they had spied out, saying, "The land through which we have gone as spies is a land that devours its inhabitants, and all the people whom we saw in it are men of great stature." There we saw the giants (the descendants of Anak came from the giants); and we were like grasshoppers in our own sight, and so we were in their sight.

Here the people of God magnified the giants and minimized themselves. They allowed their emotional reasoning to take over. Assuming that our negative emotions reflect the way things really are is harmful and destructive. In other words, we are saying, "I feel it; therefore it must be true." Remember that Caleb and Joshua were seeing grapes while everybody else was seeing giants. Again, self talk is not about ignoring a problem or pretending it doesn't exist, but it's about standing on the promise that God has already given us the victory and not allowing ourselves to magnify or minimize our circumstances.

The seventh distortion of twisted thinking involves making "should" statements. "I should do this," or "I should do that," or "You should have done that," and, "You should have done this." You're headed for trouble when you start should-ing on yourself. These "should" statements issue negative judgments about your actions and behaviors and produce the consequence of guilt. Don't do it.

Paul refers to this twisted thinking pattern when he warns the Corinthians against worldly sorrow. Second Corinthians 7:10 says, "For godly sorrow produces repentance leading to salvation, not to be regretted; but the sorrow of the world produces death." Paul Meyer suggests the most useless time thief of all is regret. Meyer asks, "What if you could go back and change or make right the things you did wrong? Think of the valuable lessons we have learned from making mistakes and learning from them. Are we going to regret that too? 'I should' produces guilt. 'You should' produces anger, frustration, and resentment."

I have found myself doing this "should" thing with God. God should do this, and God should have done that. We find ourselves struggling and fighting with God instead of trusting Him. Take responsibility, but then confess it to God. Repent of it, and ask God to take the mess and turn it into a miracle. Don't just keep feeling guilty. I know many parents who struggle with their children because of what they should have done when the children were young. As an old saying goes, "When is the best time to plant a tree? Twenty years ago."

When's the second best time to plant a tree? Today! Yes, you should have started positively affirming them when they were young. But stop should-ing and could-ing and would-ing, and say, "God, from today forward I'm going to make a transformation in how I communicate." Begin by putting your arms around your child and saying, "Please forgive me." None of us are perfect. None of us had children that came with directions. This is the personality you have been given.

The final pattern of twisted thinking is personalization or blame. This occurs when we blame ourselves for something that doesn't always prove to be entirely our fault, or we blame others without looking at ways in which our own behaviors or attitudes contributed to the problem. You can personalize a problem. You can take all the responsibility for it, but sometimes there are other people involved. You may not have been the only person responsible. I believe that one person can change a marriage, and one person can change the pace of a relationship. At some point the other person may finally see your willingness and your heart and your servanthood in attempting to make things work. Eventually, they have to step up and say, "Yes, we're going to be on the same page." But if that doesn't happen, you can't go through the rest of your life blaming yourself because of a divorce.

Parents, you can't blame yourself because an adult child has chosen to make decisions that are ruining their lives and destroying your heart. You cannot do that. Please don't personalize everything and say, "It's all my fault!" There are other issues involved so many times. The other side of that coin is don't blame others without taking your part of the responsibility.

A great story in Exodus 18 illustrates this point. Moses was trying to lead and judge all of the Israelites and do everything himself. His father-in-law came to him and said, "Moses, what you're doing is not a good thing." It's not a good thing to judge the people and teach them the statutes of God? It wasn't a good thing for Moses to have a self-absorbed, misguided mindset that he alone could do all the teaching and judging himself. He needed the help of others.

In my office I keep Saxon White Kessinger's poem entitled "Indispensable Man."

> Sometime when you're feeling important;
> Sometime when your ego's in bloom;
> Sometime when you take it for granted,

You're the best qualified in the room:
Sometime when you feel that your going, Would leave
an unfillable hole,
Just follow these simple instructions,
And see how they humble your soul.
Take a bucket and fill it with water,
Put your hand in it up to the wrist,
Pull it out and the hole that's remaining,
Is a measure of how much you'll be missed.
You can splash all you wish when you enter,
You may stir up the water galore,
But stop, and you'll find that in no time,
It looks quite the same as before.
The moral of this quaint example is to do just the best
that you can,
Be proud of yourself but remember,
There's no indispensable man.

ACTION POINTS

1. Do you see a negative pattern in your family history that causes you concern or fear that you will repeat the process?

2. Which areas of "twisted thinking" do you struggle with the most? Which area do you struggle with the least?

3. Have you ever "should-ed" on yourself or others?

CHAPTER 14

Truth

ARE YOU READY to be a leader and mentor for truth in your own life and in the lives of others? The words that we speak breathe life. Make a commitment today to be a carrier and warrior for truth.

This Christ life cannot be lived alone. Our misguided mindsets might lead us to think that we can. The Christian life must be lived together. That's the reason we have corporate worship, corporate gathering, Bible teaching on Sunday and Wednesday, and connection in small groups. We need other people to come along side of us in life. When you are messing up, other believers need to step up and say, "Here's what God wants to do in your life." You need people in your life who know what is in your heart, not just on your mind. Don't personalize. Don't walk through life blaming your problems on everybody else when you have to take responsibility as well. When we confess the Word of God, we confess it by faith and confidence in God. He revolutionizes our lives.

I'm asking God to help us get rid of twisted thinking and help us to move away from over-generalizing everything and jumping to conclusions. *God, help us to move to what the Bible says. Let us live our lives every day by bringing our motives, attitudes, words, actions, and thoughts to You. Help us to bring them into alignment with Your Word.* Do you think God can radically change us when we pray this? I know He can.

I have a "Top Ten Never-Again" list. I use the list and the Scriptures on a daily basis. Write your own top ten list and find Scriptures that relate to your life. Then every day, ask God to help you to rehearse them until they become a part of your life.

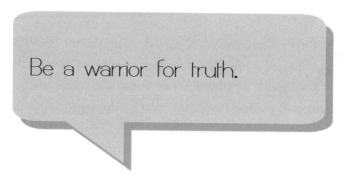

Be a warrior for truth.

TOP TEN NEVER-AGAIN LIST

1. Philippians 4—Never again will I confess I can't do something, because I can do all things through Christ who gives me the strength.

2. Philippians 4:19—Never again will I confess lack, because my God supplies all of my needs according to His riches and glory by Christ Jesus.

3. 2 Timothy 1:7—Never again will I confess fear, because God has told me that He did not give me the spirit of fear. I've got power, I've got love, I've got self.

4. Romans 12:3—Never again will I confess my doubt or lack of faith, for God said not to doubt Him. It is the measure of faith.

5. Daniel 11:32—Never again will I confess weakness, for the Bible says that the people who know their God are going to be strong.

6. 1 John 4:4—Never again will I confess the supremacy of Satan over my life, because greater is He that is in me than he that is in the world.

7. 2 Corinthians 2:14—Never again will I confess defeat, for the Bible says God is always causing me to triumph in Christ Jesus.

8. 1 Corinthians 1:30—Never again will I confess lack of wisdom, for Christ was made the wisdom of God.

9. Isaiah 53:5—Never again will I confess sickness, because with His stripes I am healed.

10. 1 Peter 5:7—Never again will I confess worries or doubt, because every day I cast my care upon Him, and He cares for me.

When you find yourself confessing lack, fear, and the

supremacy of Satan, when you find yourself confessing worry and doubt, remind yourself to bring your motives, attitudes, thoughts, words, and actions into alignment with God's Word. "Lord, who shall abide in thy tabernacle? Who shall dwell in thy holy hill? He that walketh uprightly, and worketh in righteousness, *and speaketh the truth in his heart*" (Psalm 15:1–2). The Bible will be your best source for finding help and truth.

We are overcomers in Christ Jesus. We are more than conquerors in Him. Grab these truths and apply them in your family, your life, your job, and your finances. Decide to get rid of your twisted thinking and build your life on God's Word for the rest of your life by bringing every thought into captivity to Him. Speaking God's life-changing words into your life will activate your faith positively. In the process you will turn the self-imposed words of death into words of life.

ACTION POINTS

1. Who do you have in your life right now who will hold you accountable to be a carrier of truth for yourself and others?

2. Ask a friend or spouse these questions concerning the self talk they hear coming from you:

   • What is one thing I need to stop doing?

   • What is one thing I need to start doing?

   • What is one thing I need to keep doing?

3. Write down the top ten positive declarations that God would say to describe you and your life. Read these declarations daily for a week.

Resources

Eldredge, John. *Wild at Heart*. Nashville, Tennessee: Thomas Nelson, 2001, 2010.

Gerald, Kevin. *Forces That Form Your Future*. Tacoma, Washington: KGC Publishing, 2003, 2011.

Lloyd-Jones, David Martyn. *Spiritual Depression: Its Causes and Its Cure*. Grand Rapids, Michigan: Eerdmans Printing Company, 1965.

Maxwell, John. *Thinking for a Change*. New York, New York: Warner Books, Inc., 2003.

Maxwell, John. *Today Matters*. New York, New York: Time Warner Book Group, 2004.

Meyers, Joyce. *Managing Your Emotions*. Fenton, Missouri: Life in the Word, Inc.,1997.

Osteen, Joel. *Your Best Life Now*. New York, New York: Hatchette Book Group, USA, 2004.

Online Resources

http://westsidetoastmasters.com/resources/laws_persuasion/
chap8.html

http://www.bodymindspiritonline.com/bodymindspirit/
edition17/12_article_jack.html

http://www.sharefaith.com/guide/Christian-Music/
hymns-the-songs-and-the-stories/it-is-well-with-my-soul-the-
song-and-the-story.html

http://www.bragg.army.mil/directorates/chaplain/chapels/
woodmemorialchapel

http://www.dailymail.co.uk/sciencetech/article-2281891/
Women-really-talk-men. html

http://www.loveandlogic.com

http://www.biography.com/people/beverly-sills-9483761

http://en.wikipedia.org/wiki/Play-Doh